INSPIRING COLORING BOOK FOR ADULTS WITH QUOTES
VOLUME I / III

Mind full of fears, there is no place for dreams

Good vibes and uplifting messages: simple designs in large print

William Colins

© **Copyright 2020 - All rights reserved.**

The contents of this book may not be reproduced, duplicated or transmitted without direct written permission from the author. Under no circumstances will any legal responsibility or blame be held against the publisher for any reparation, damages, or monetary loss due to the information herein, either directly or indirectly.

Legal Notice:

You cannot amend, distribute, sell, use, quote or paraphrase any part of the content within this book without the consent of the author.

Disclaimer Notice:

Please note the information contained within this document is for educational and entertainment purposes only. No warranties of any kind are expressed or implied. Readers acknowledge that the author is not engaging in the rendering of legal, financial, medical or professional advice.

Introduction

Interesting book with great texts, shapes and figures, ready to start developing the coloring technique and thus do a wonderful and satisfying job with your wits.

You will implant a fortifying vision and a very interesting perspective on the opposite events of daily life, to obtain opportunities from them and grow wisely.

Really inspiring messages that positively determine a more encouraging vision for dealing with negative thoughts.

So get ready to enjoy it, read it, learn it and thus color each of its pages in the most energetic and magical way possible.

William Colins

Dedication

*With all the love in my heart to
Agustin Mateo and
Teo Alejandro*

My special thanks go to

My son, who with great dedication and care, guided me in the making of this book.

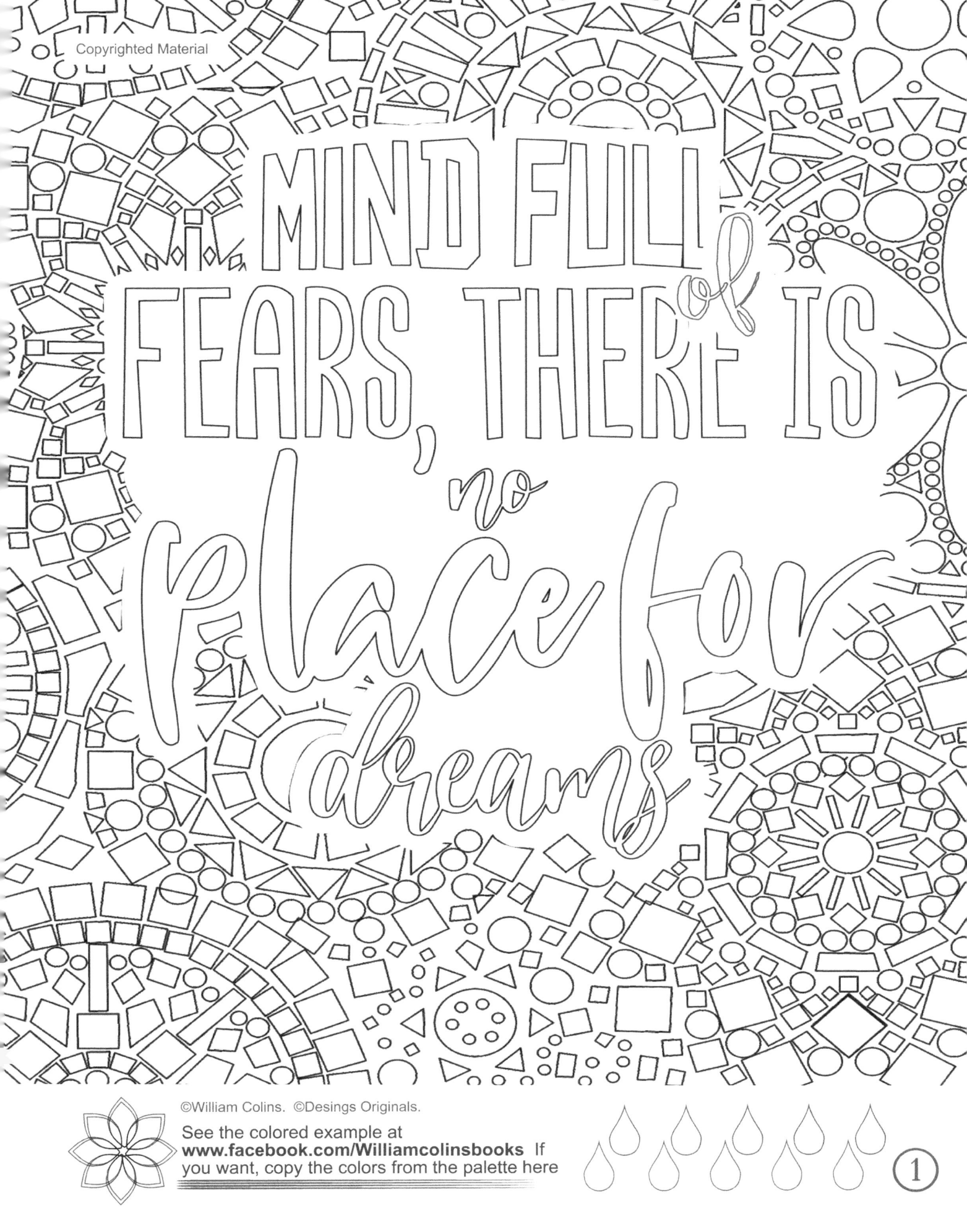

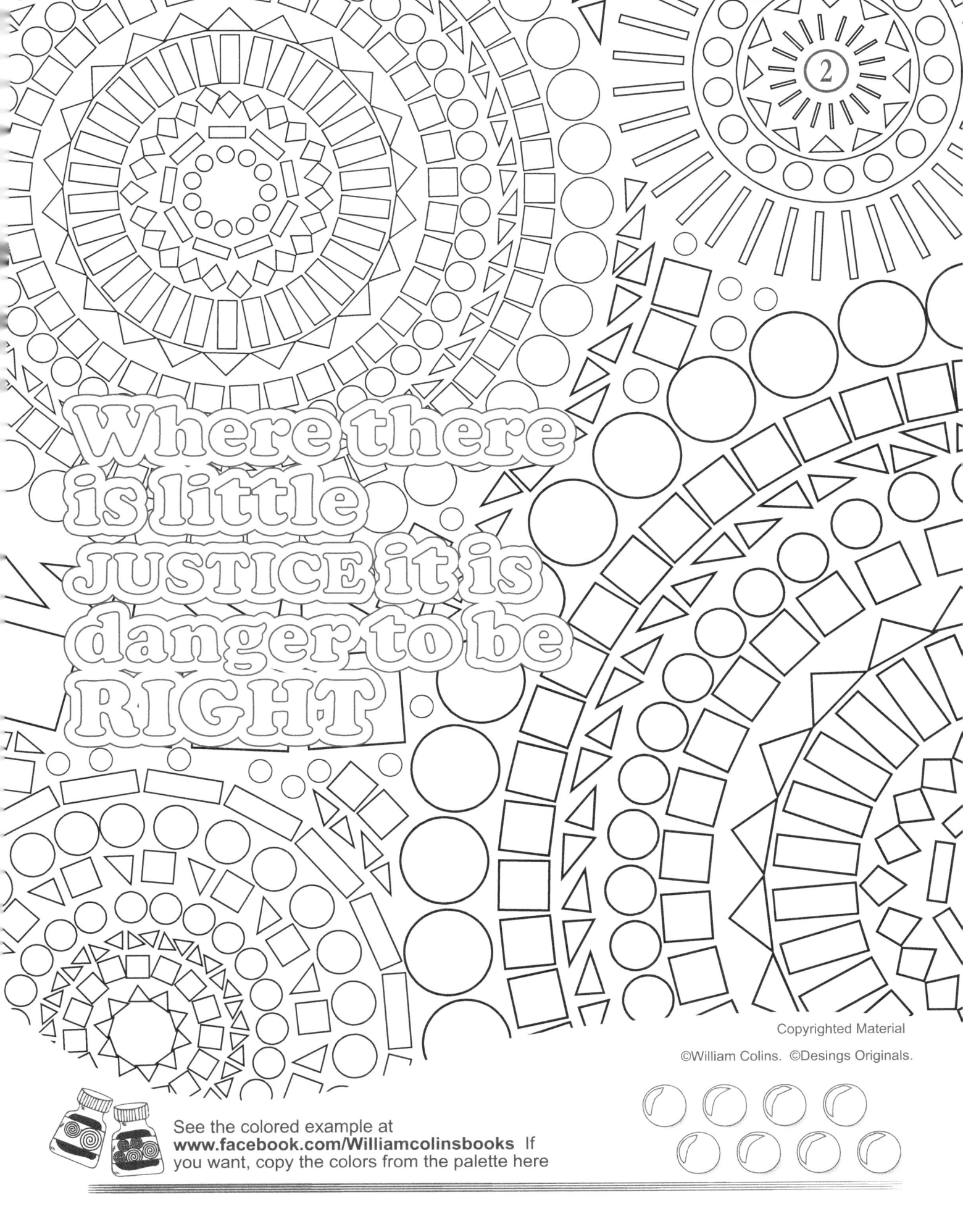

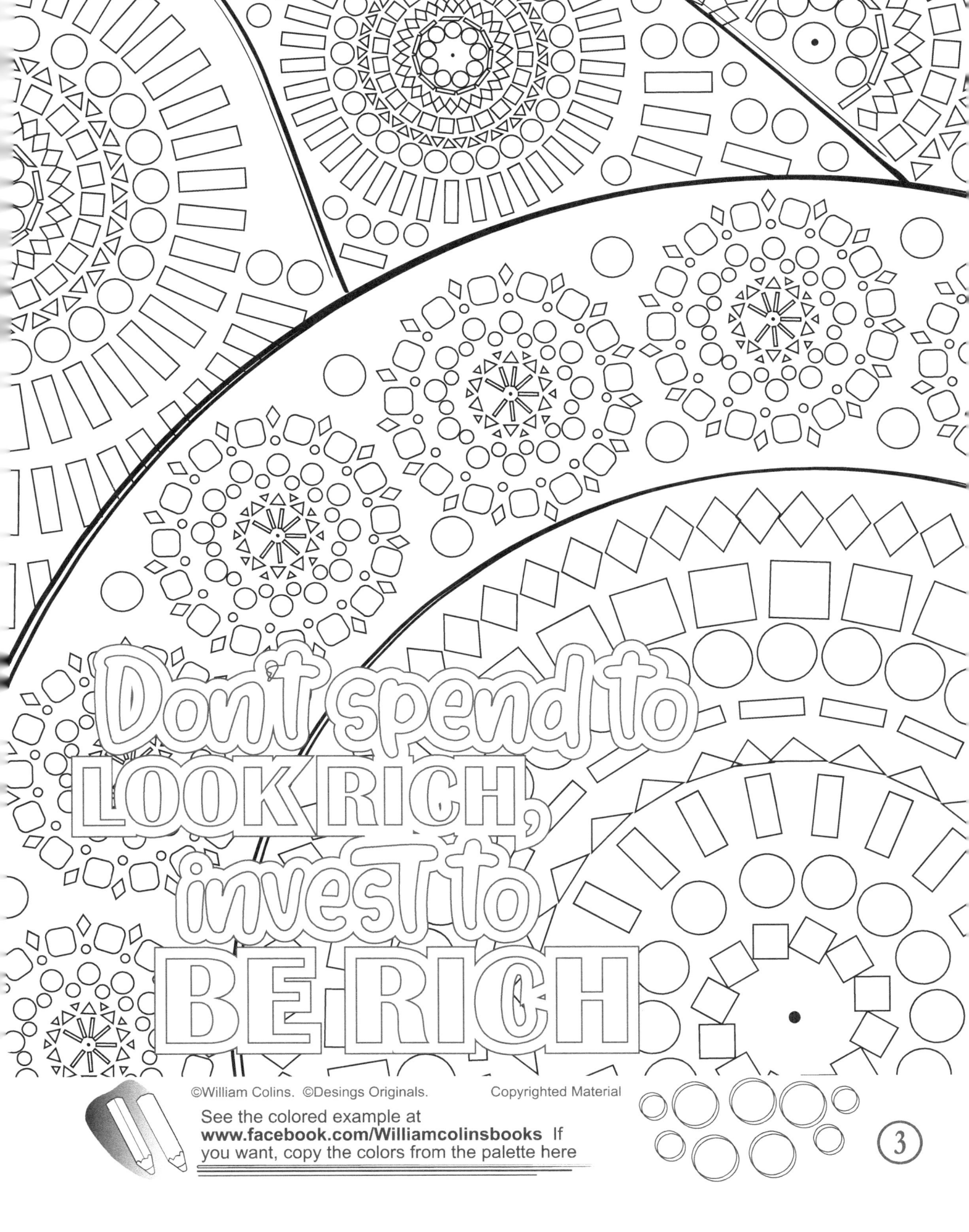

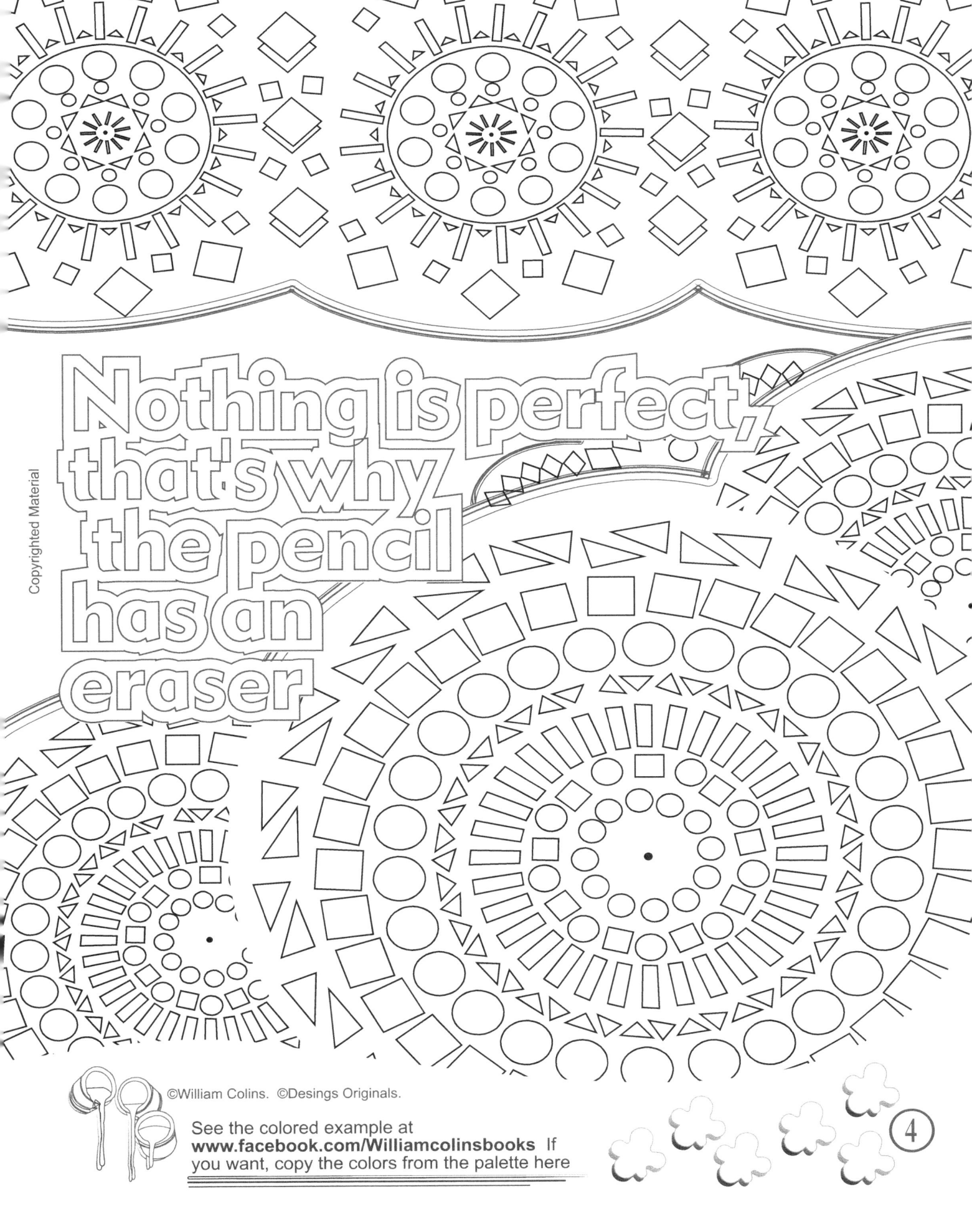

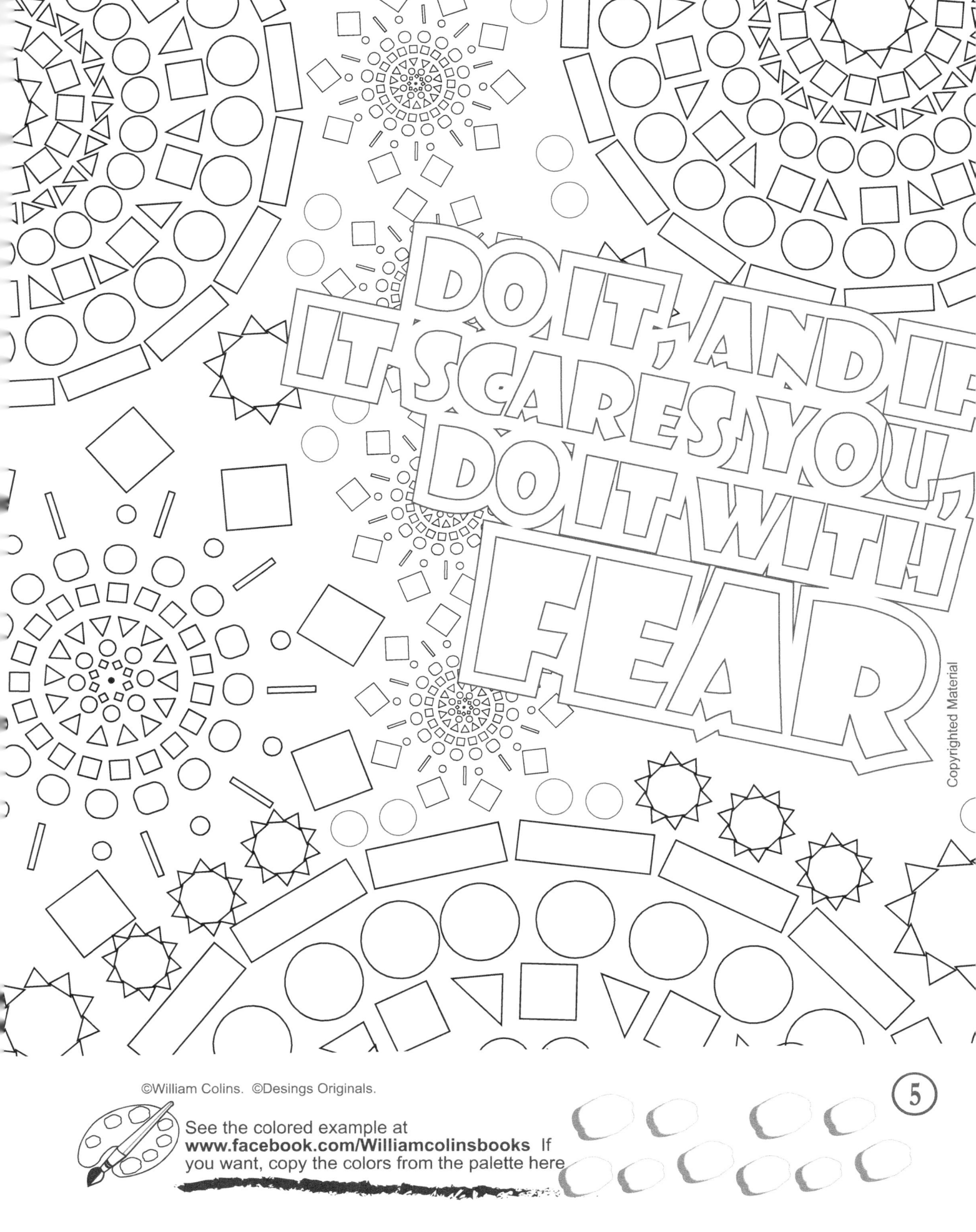

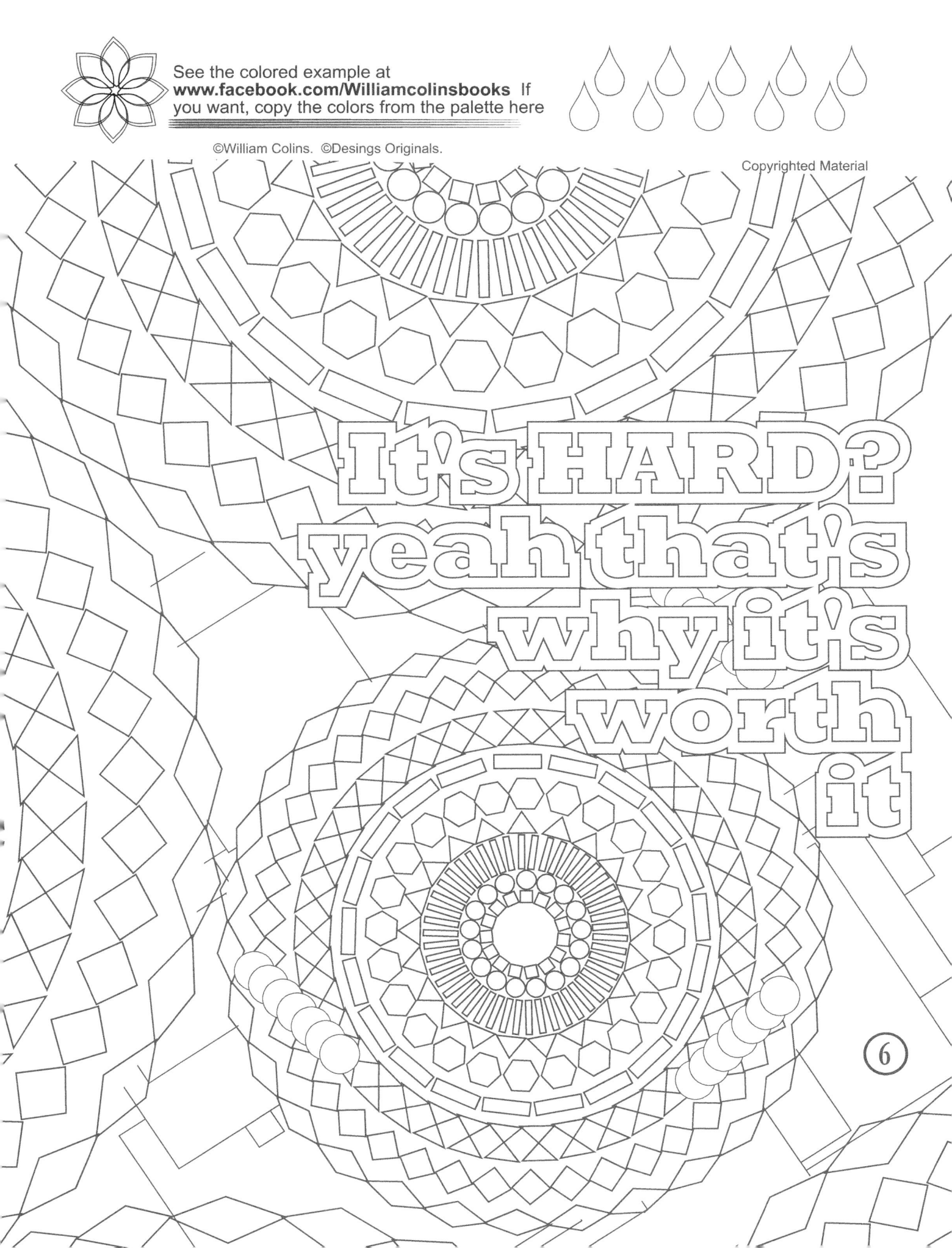

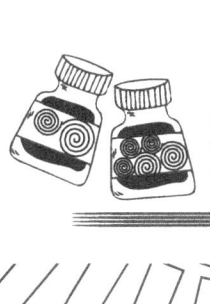 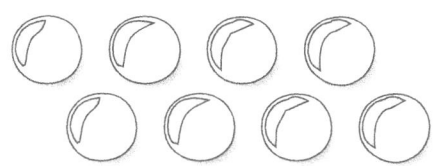

See the colored example at **www.facebook.com/WilliamColinsbooks** If you want, copy the colors from the palette here

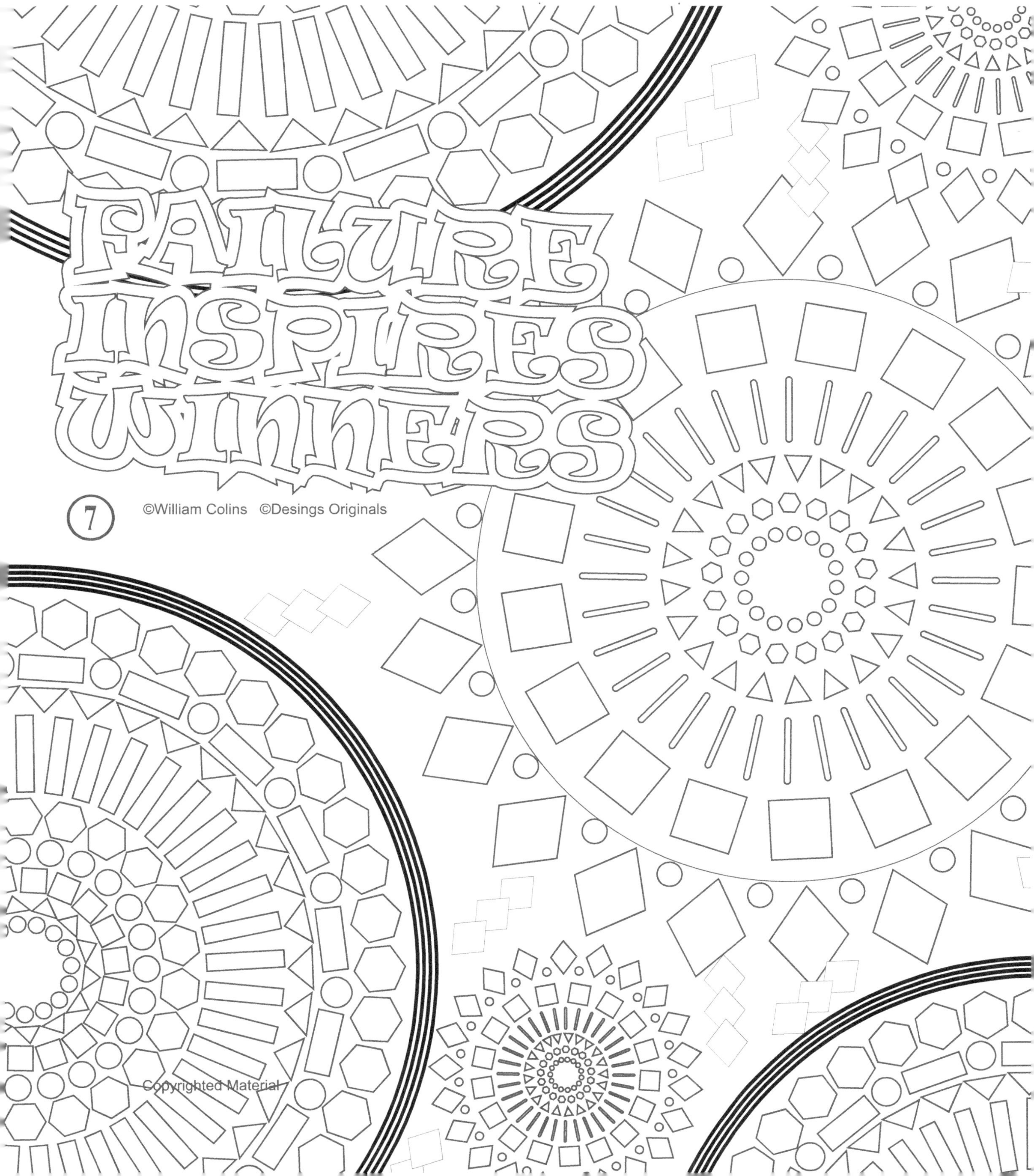

FAILURE INSPIRES WINNERS

⑦ ©William Colins ©Desings Originals

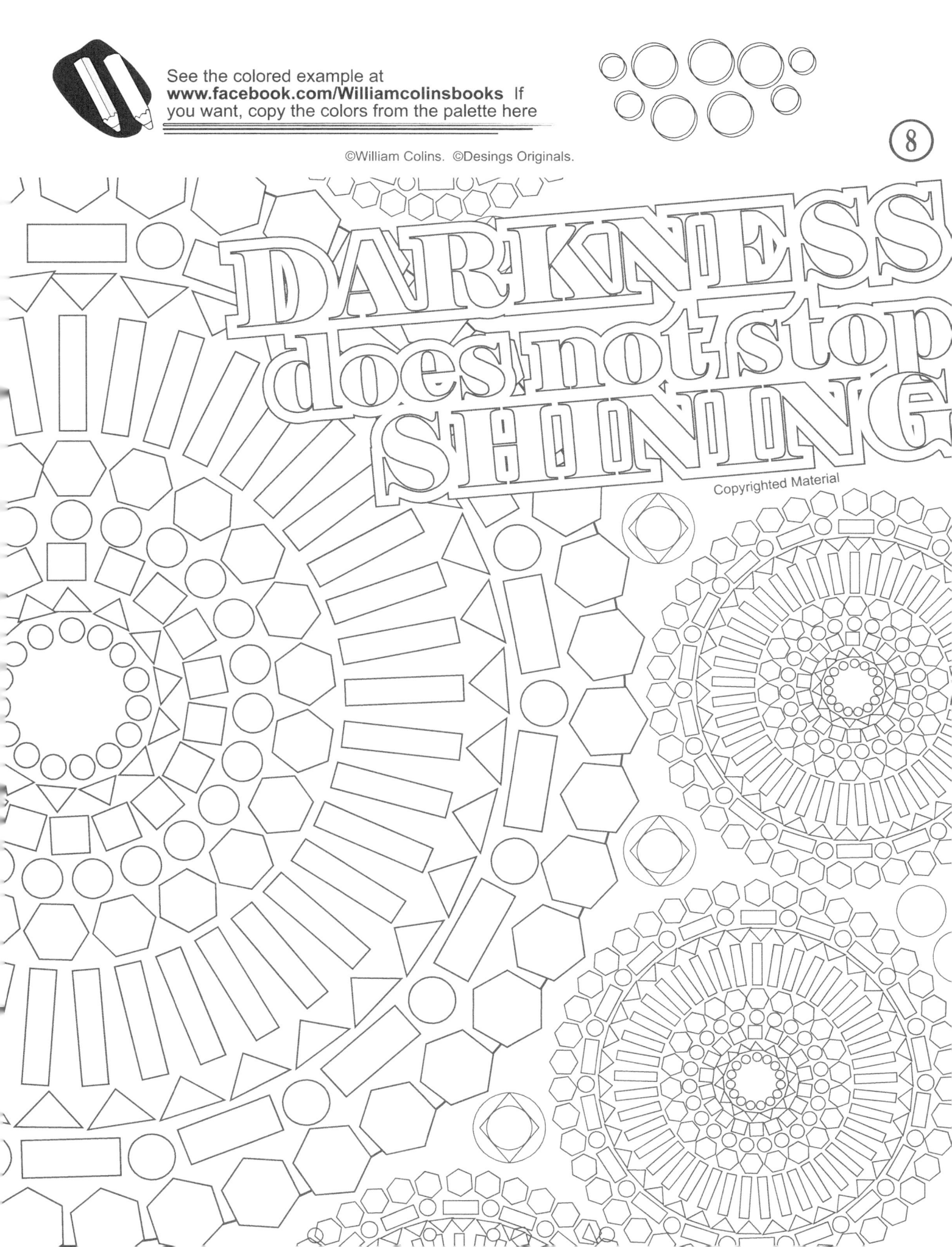

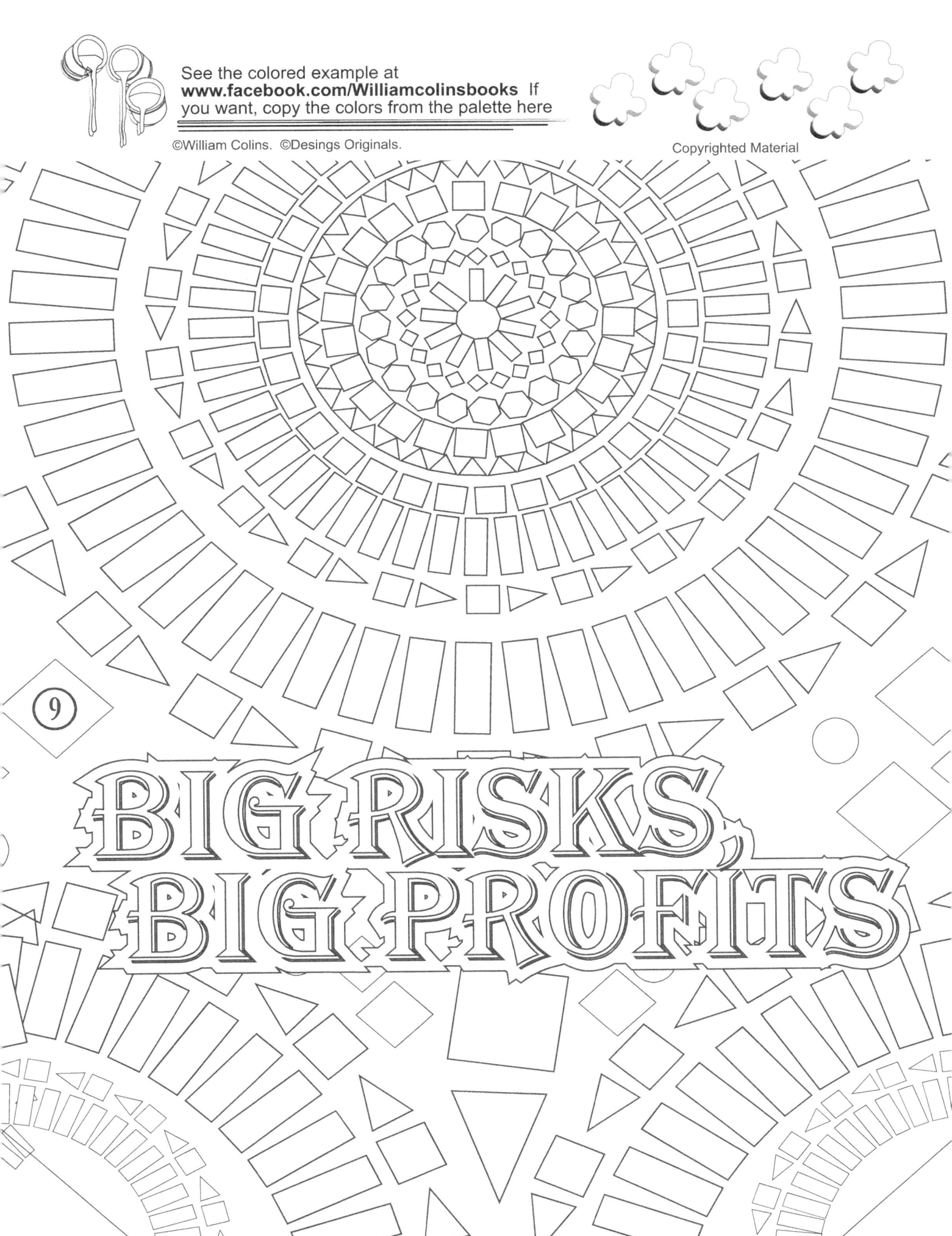

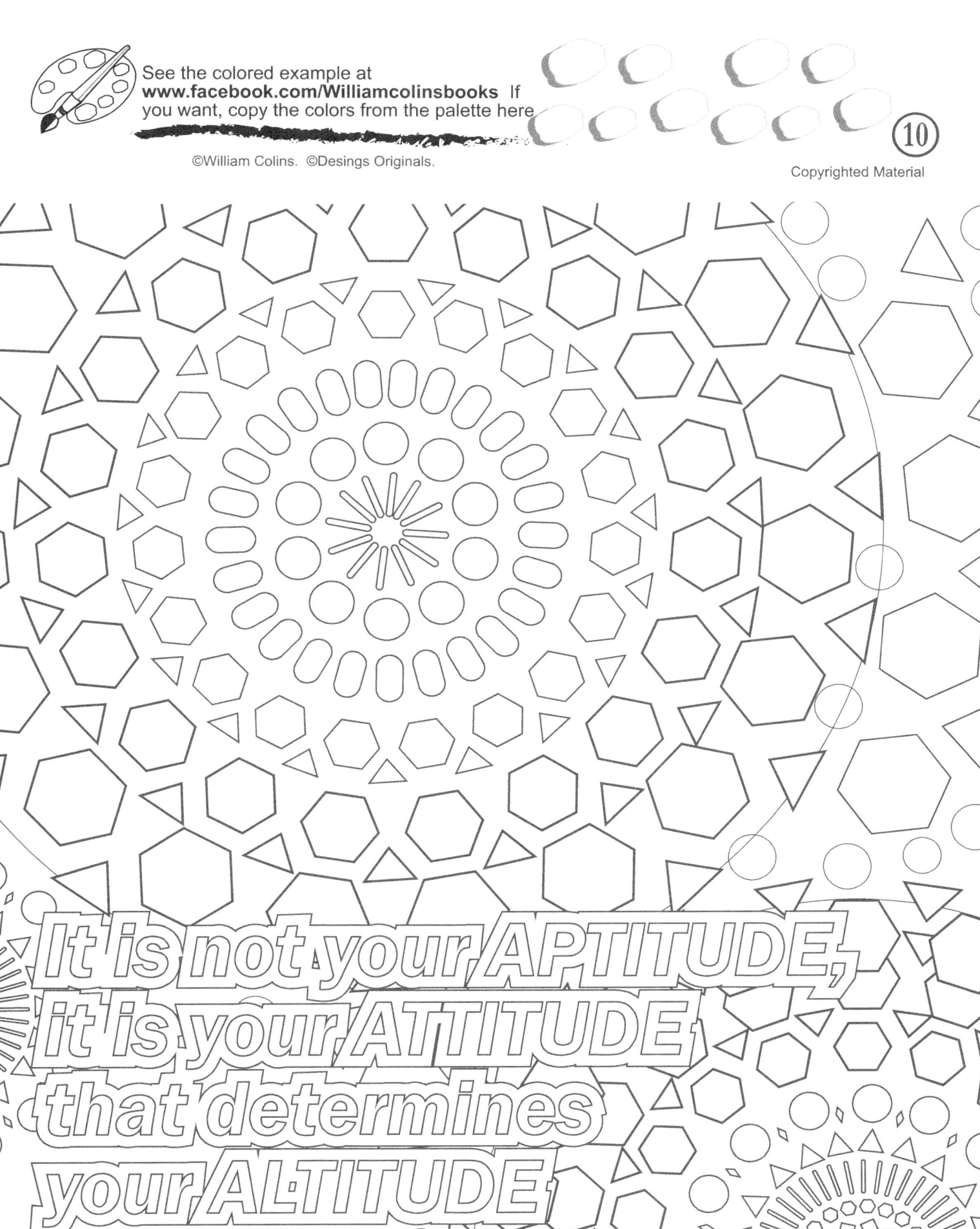

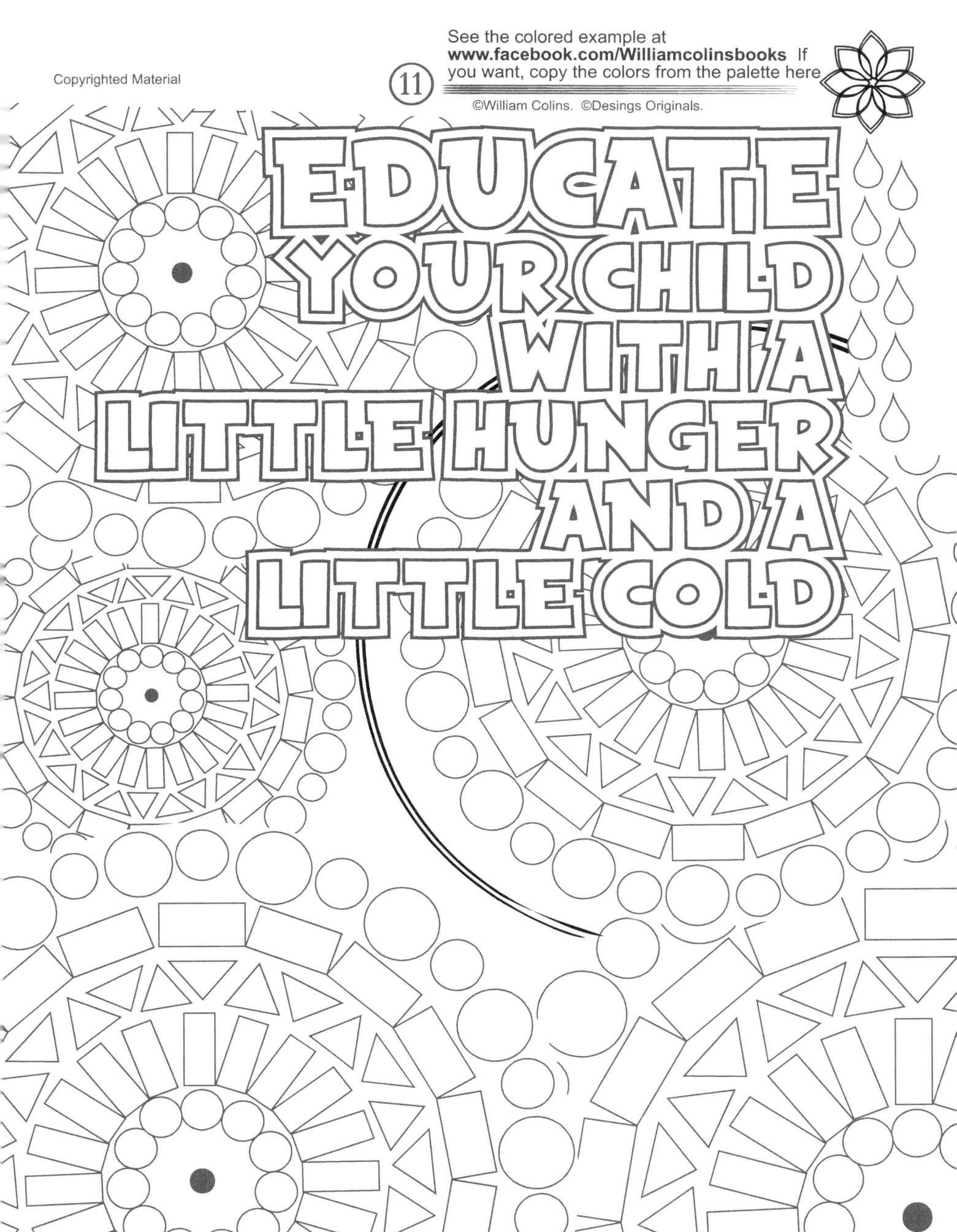

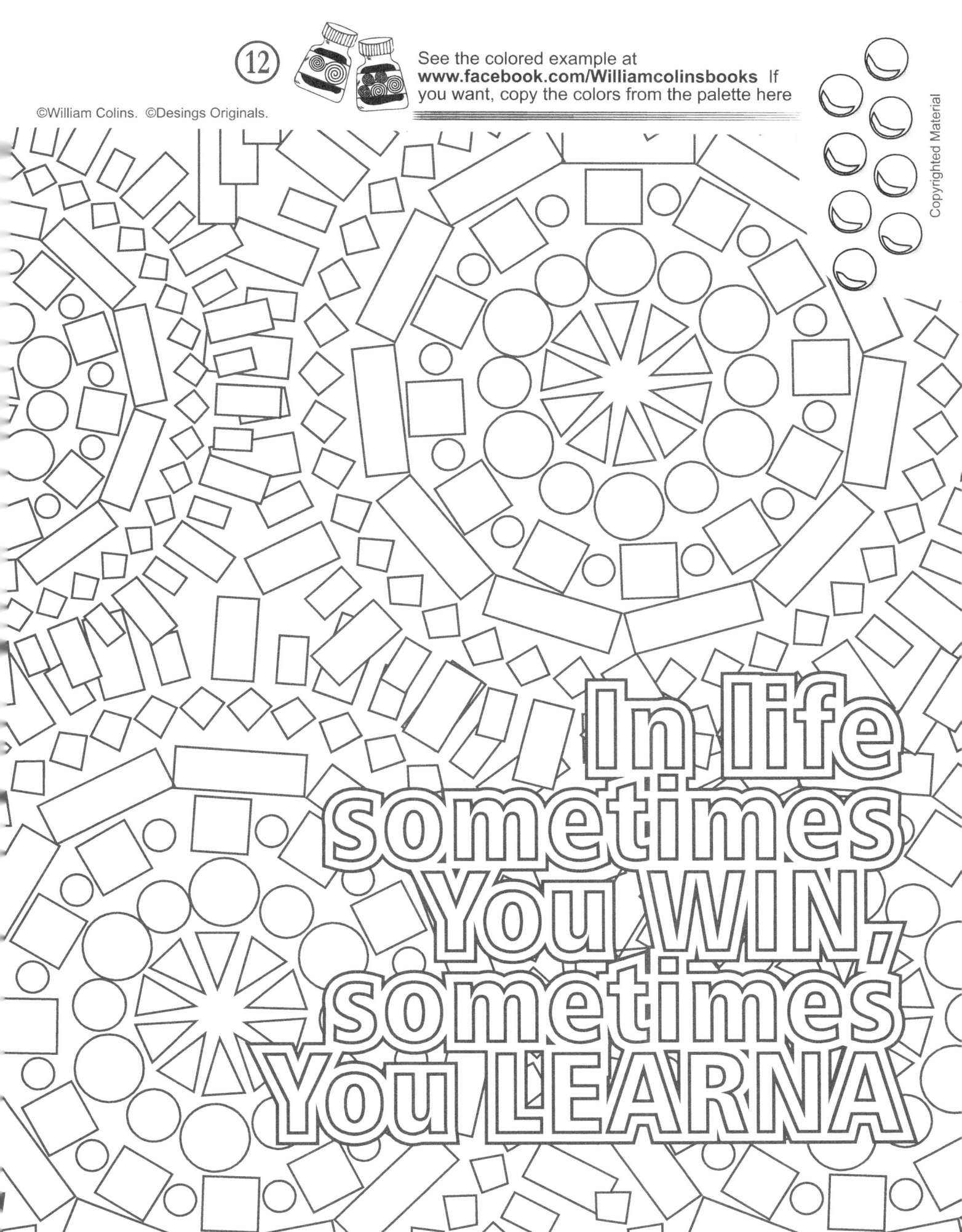

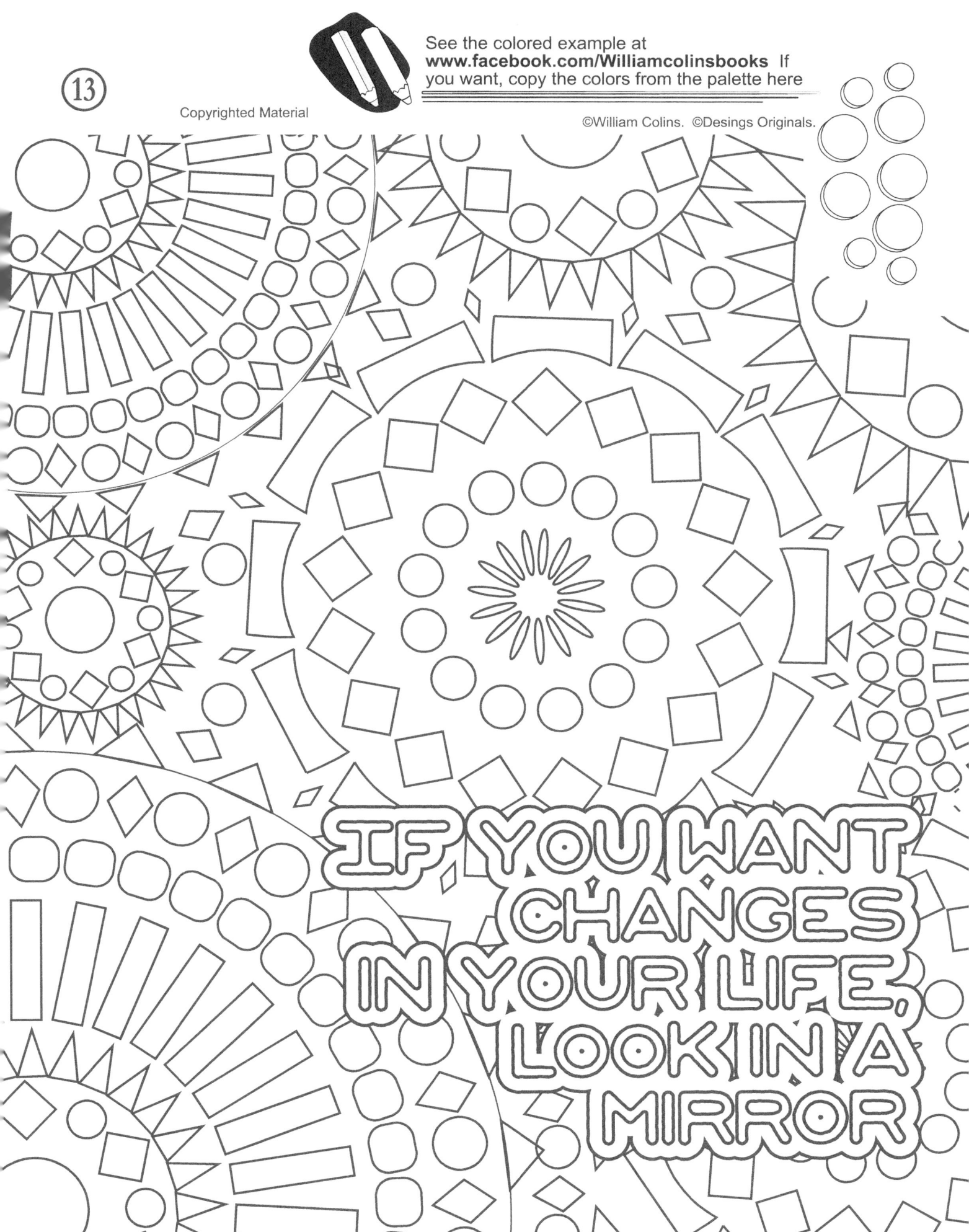

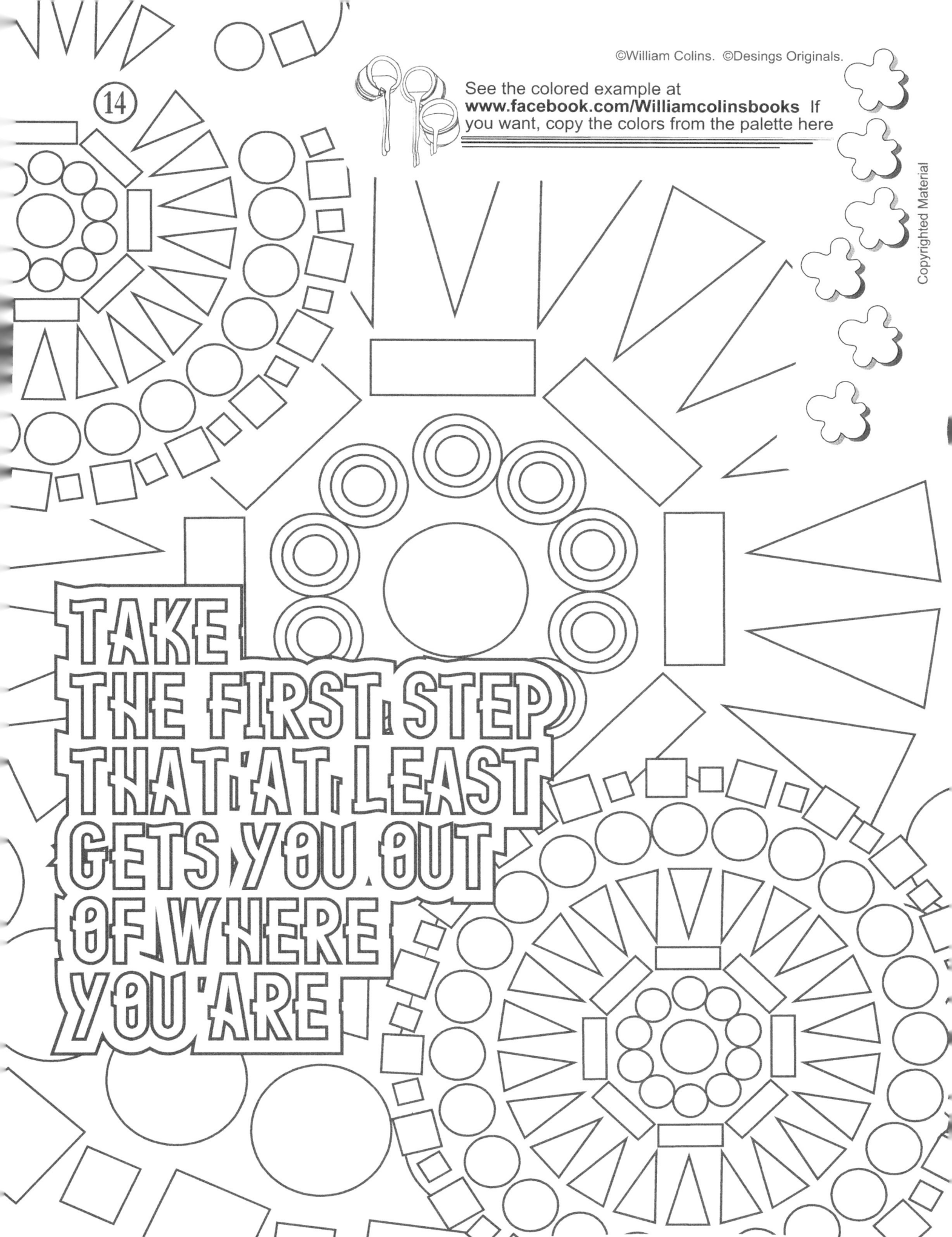

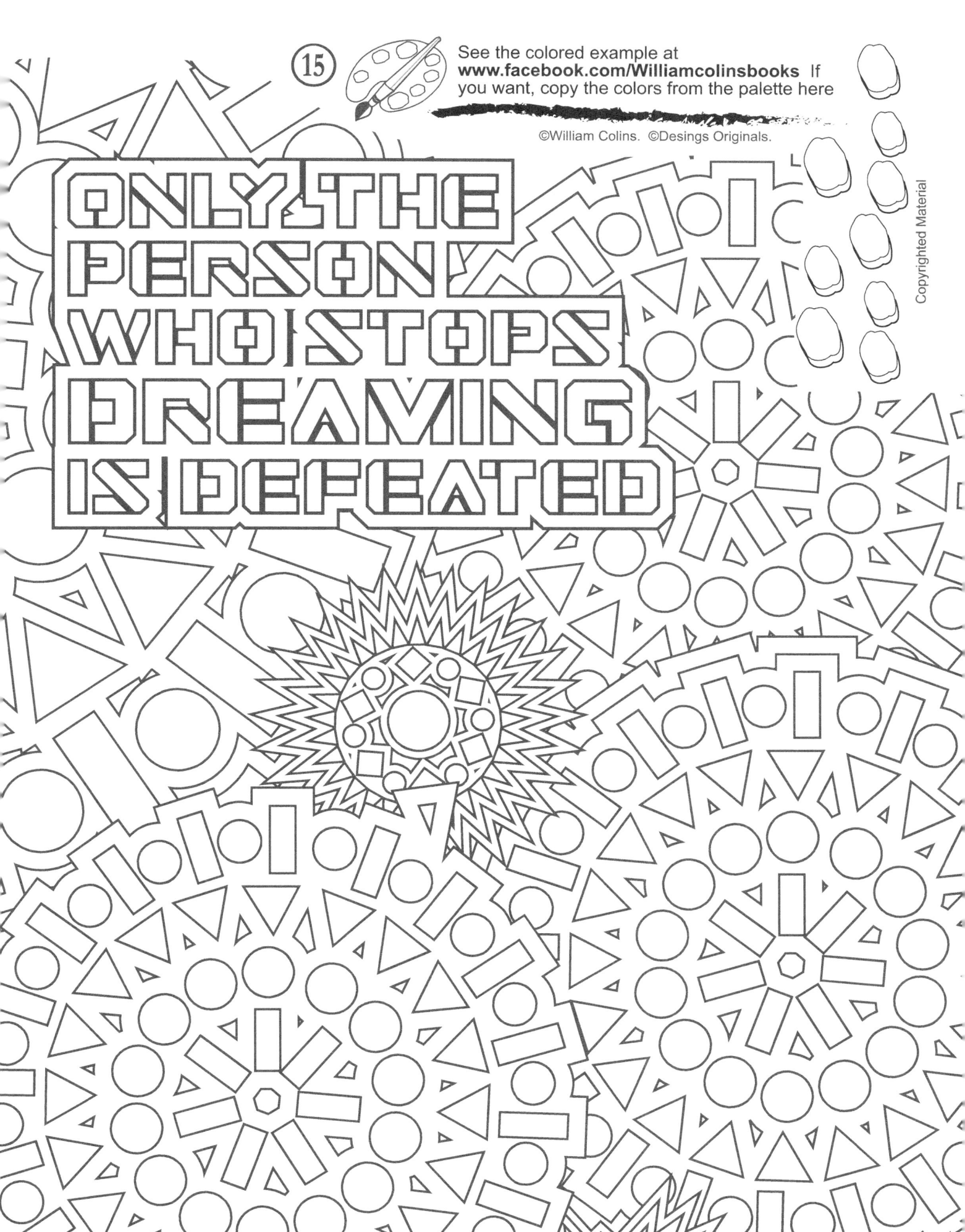

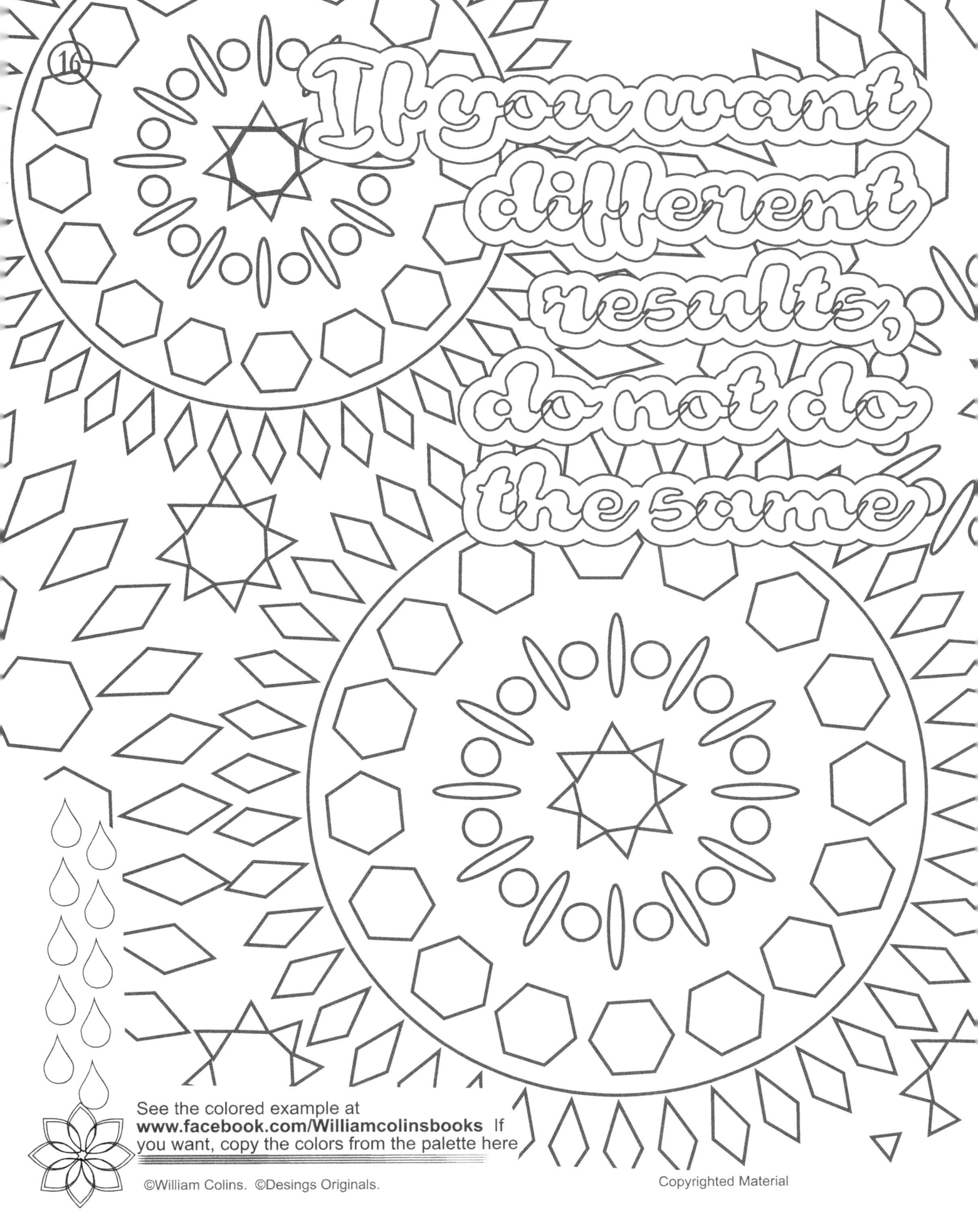

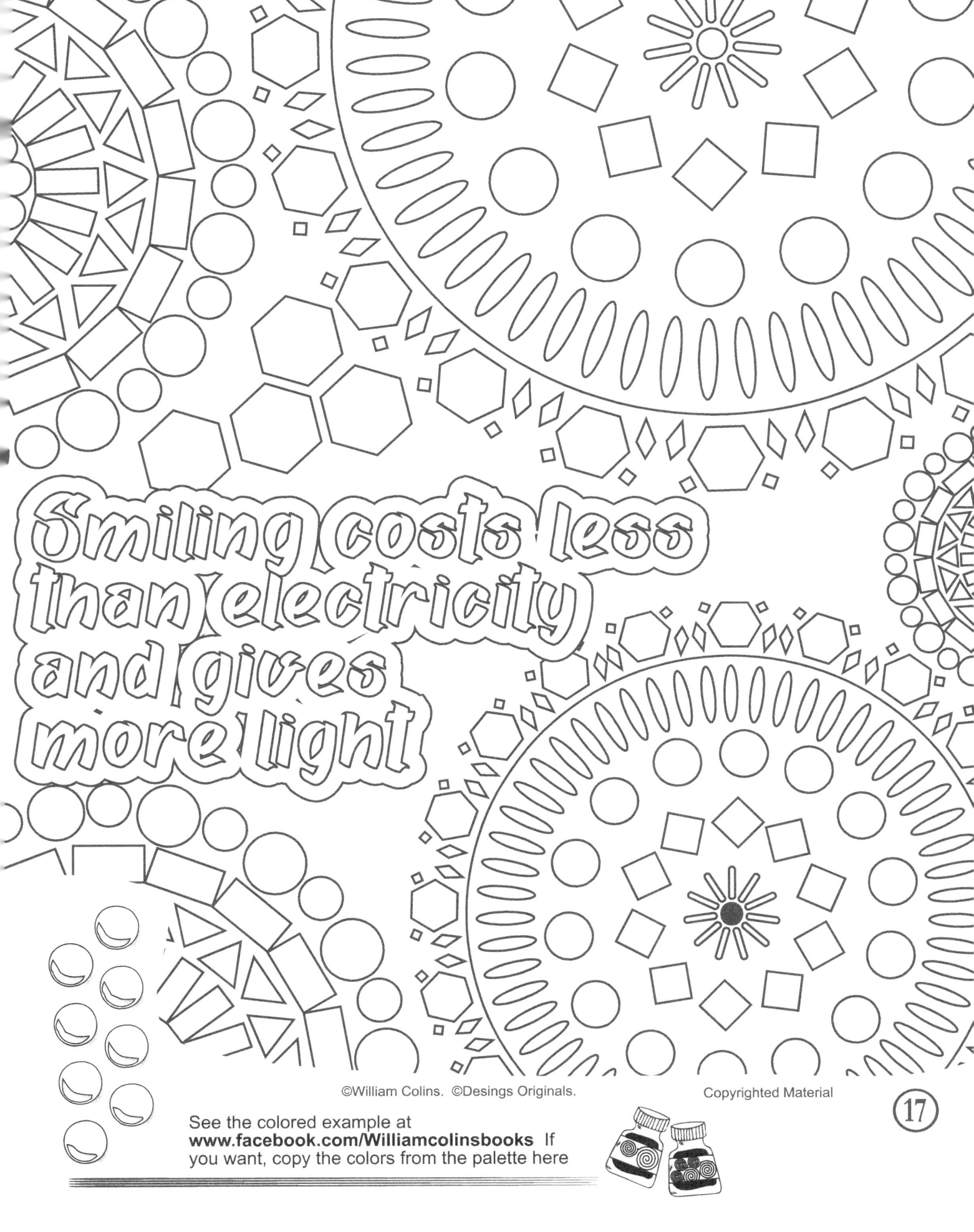

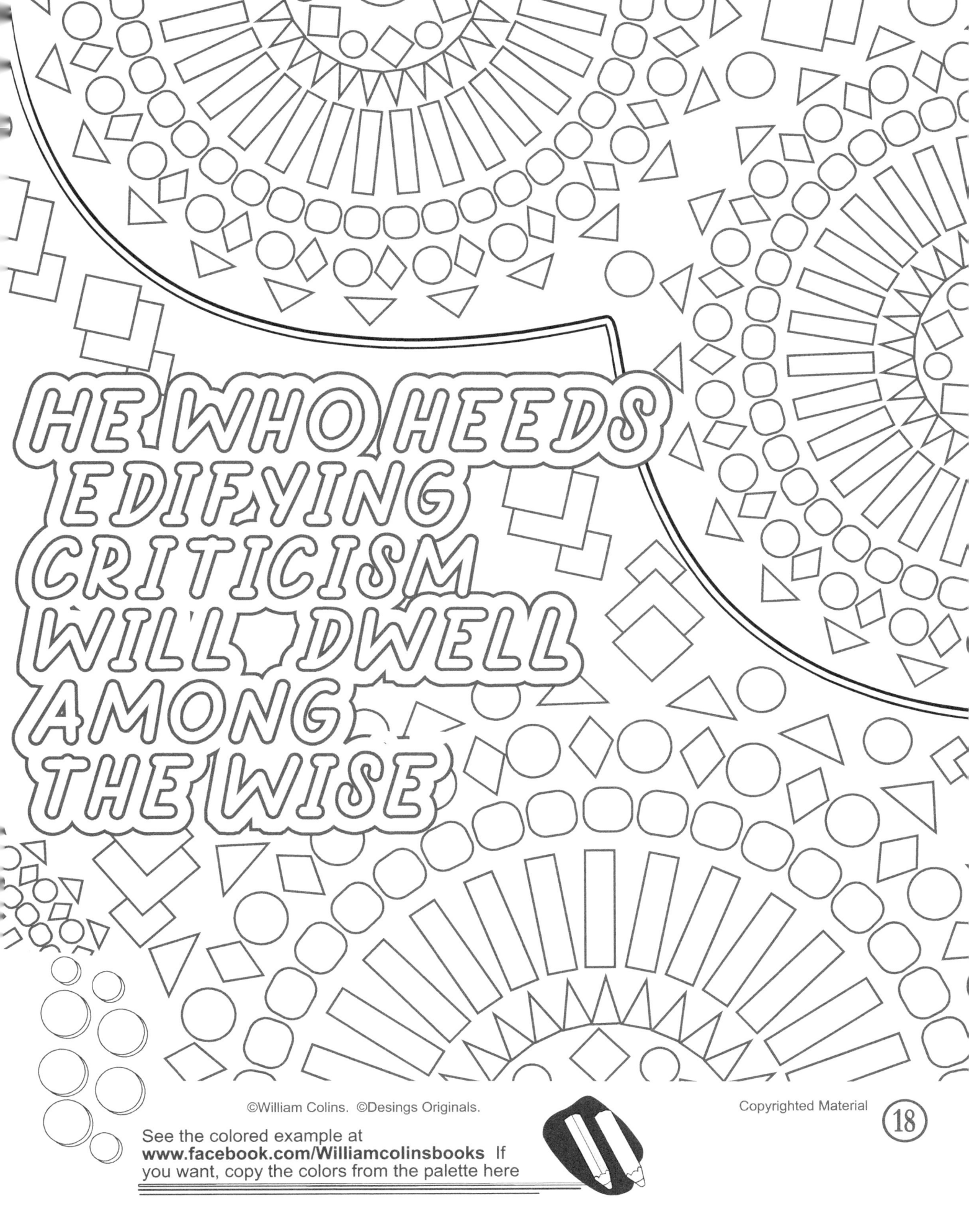

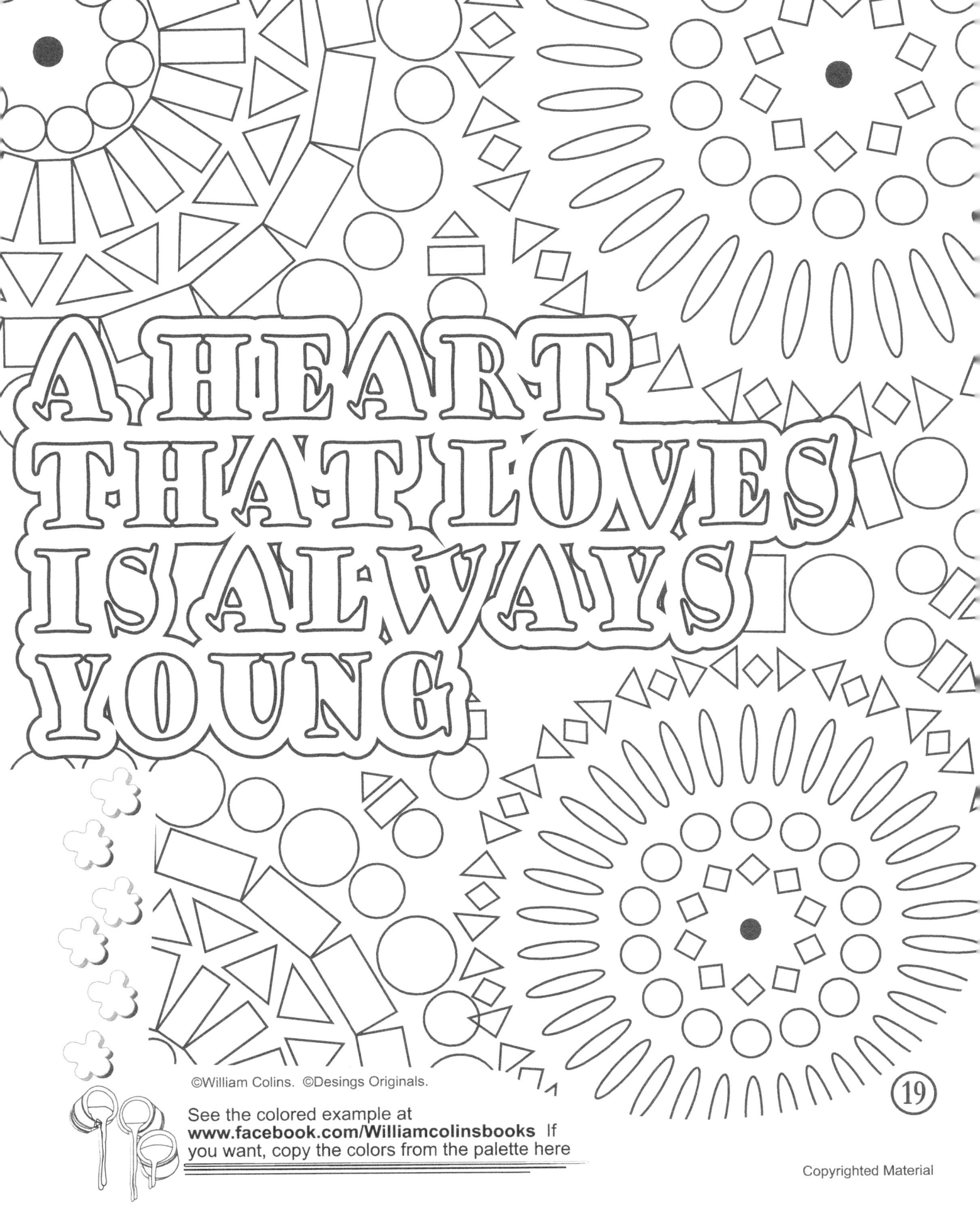

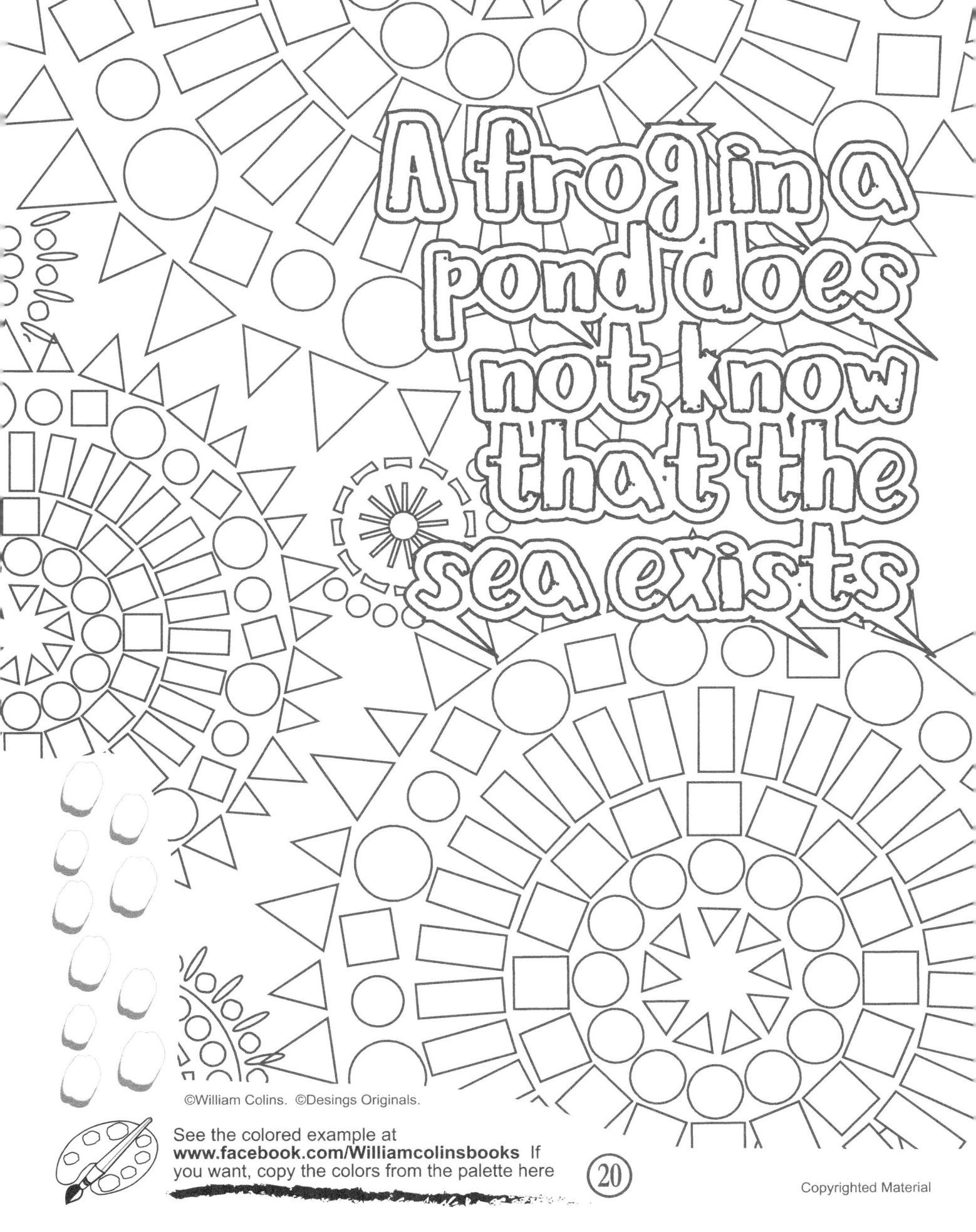

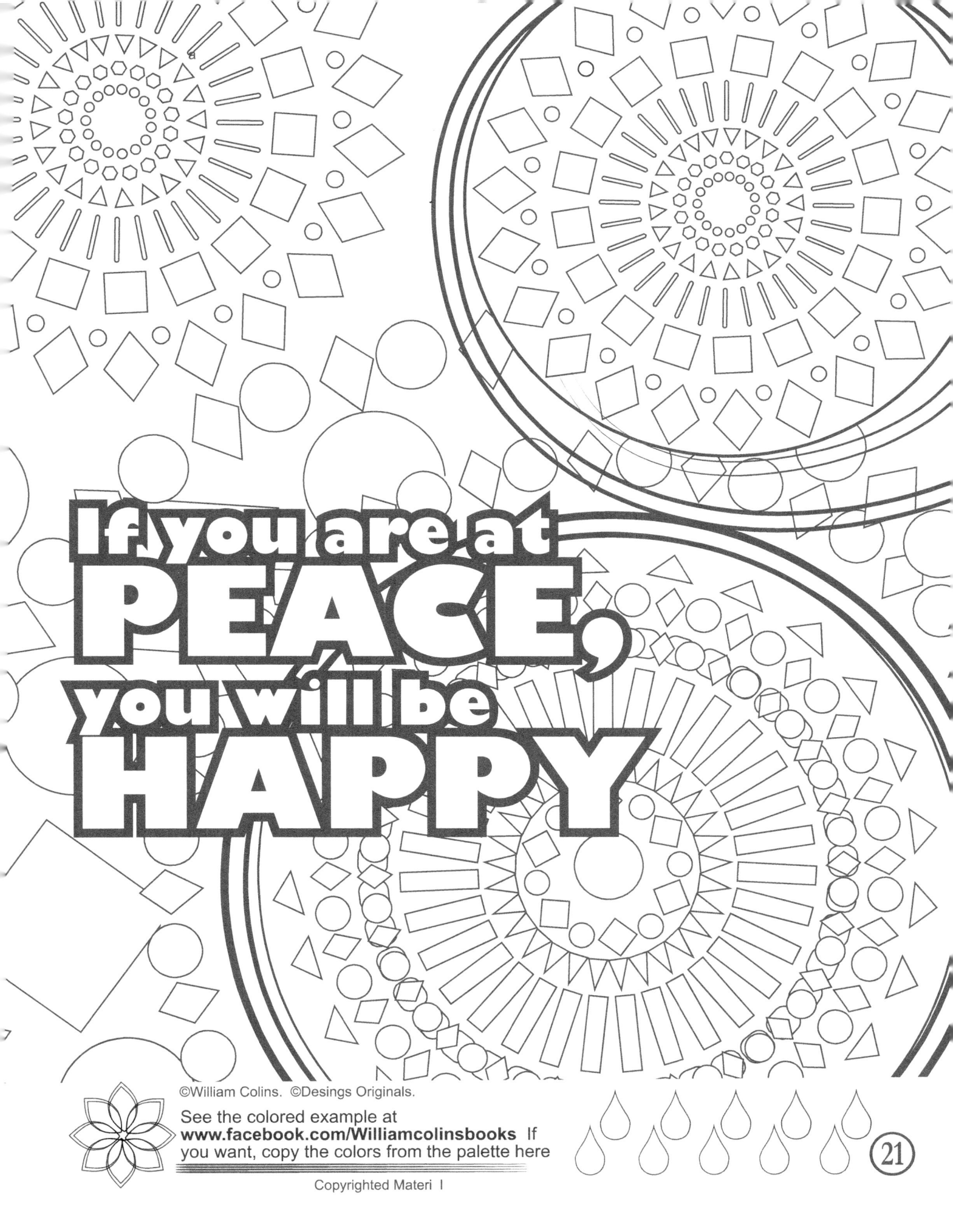

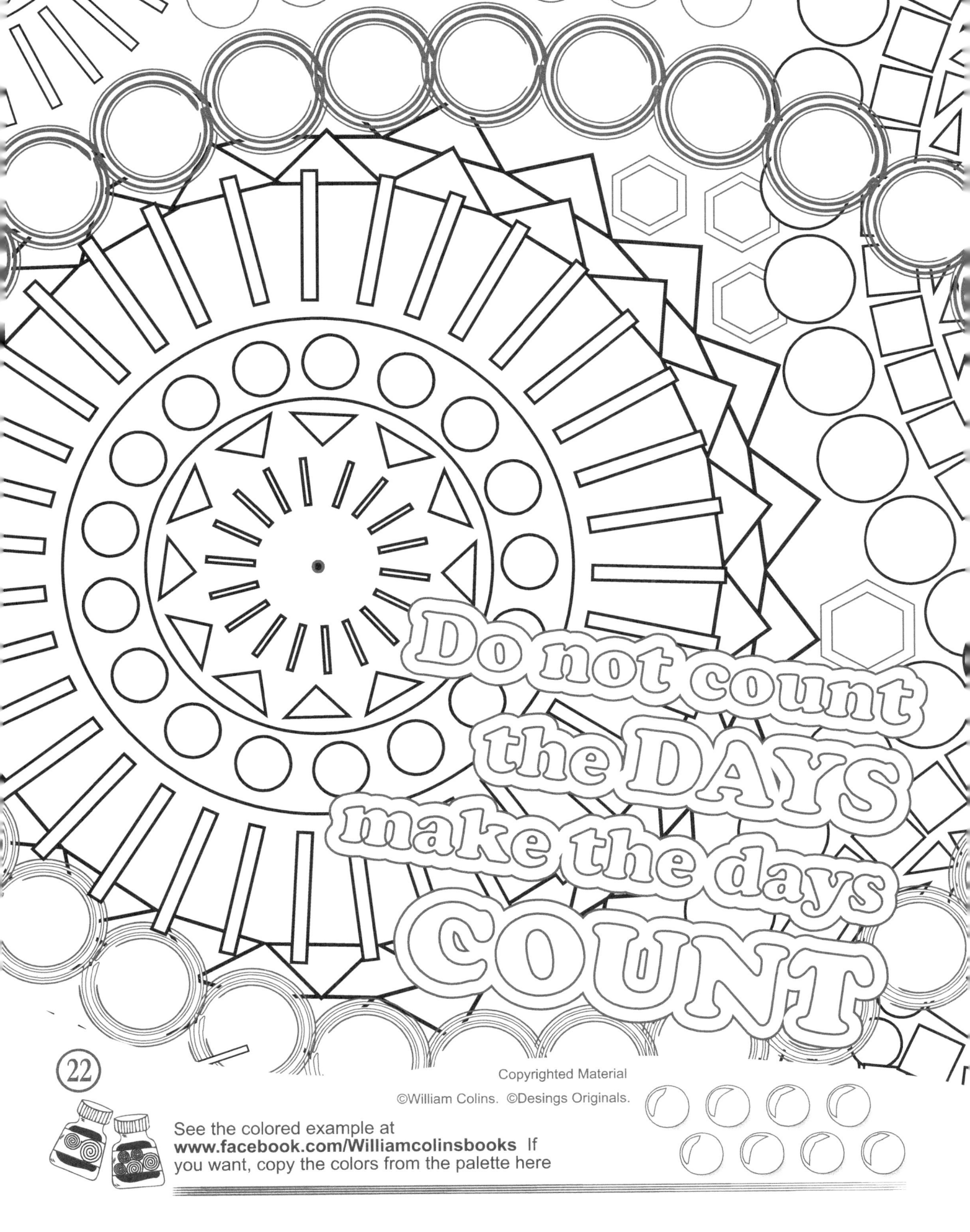

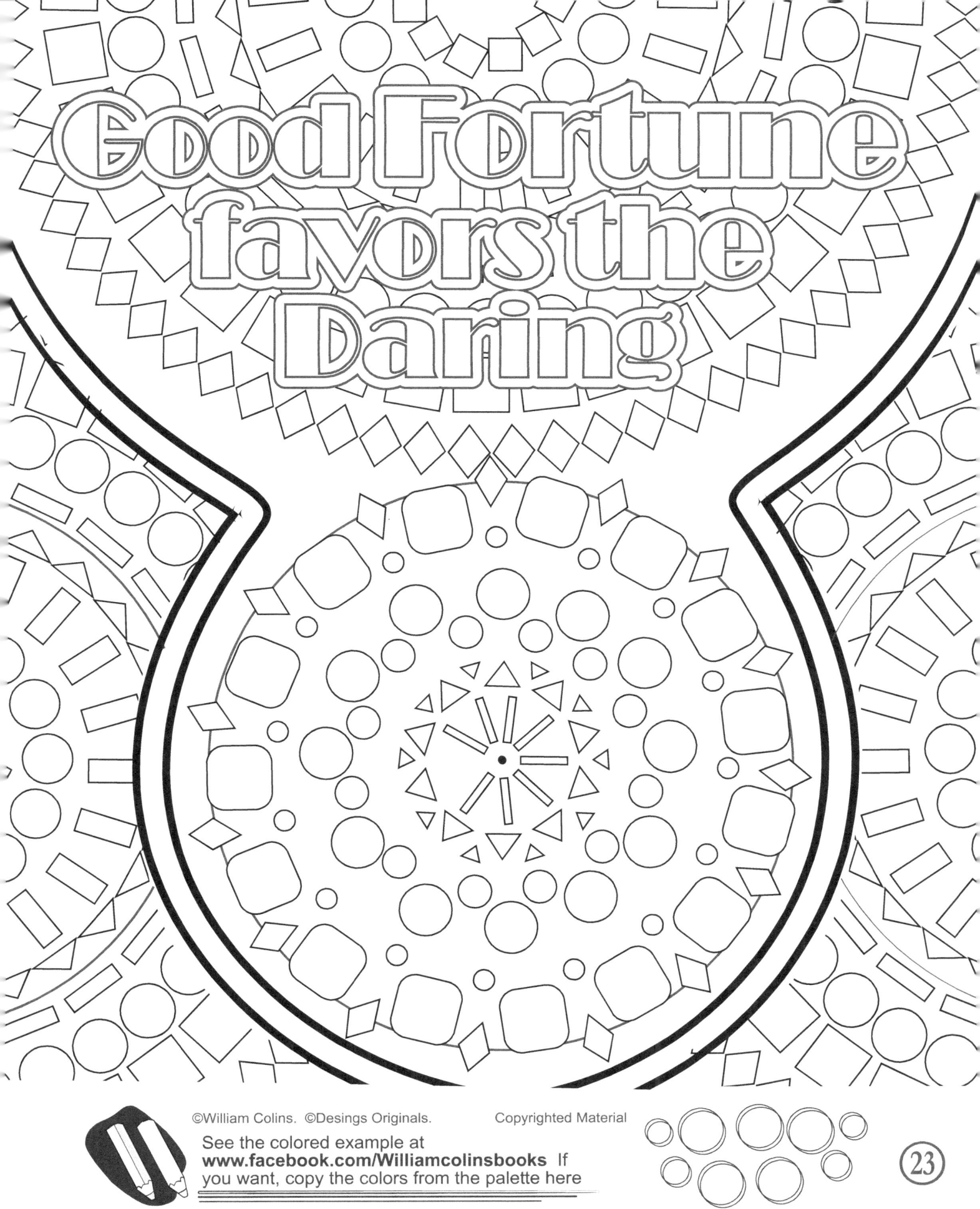

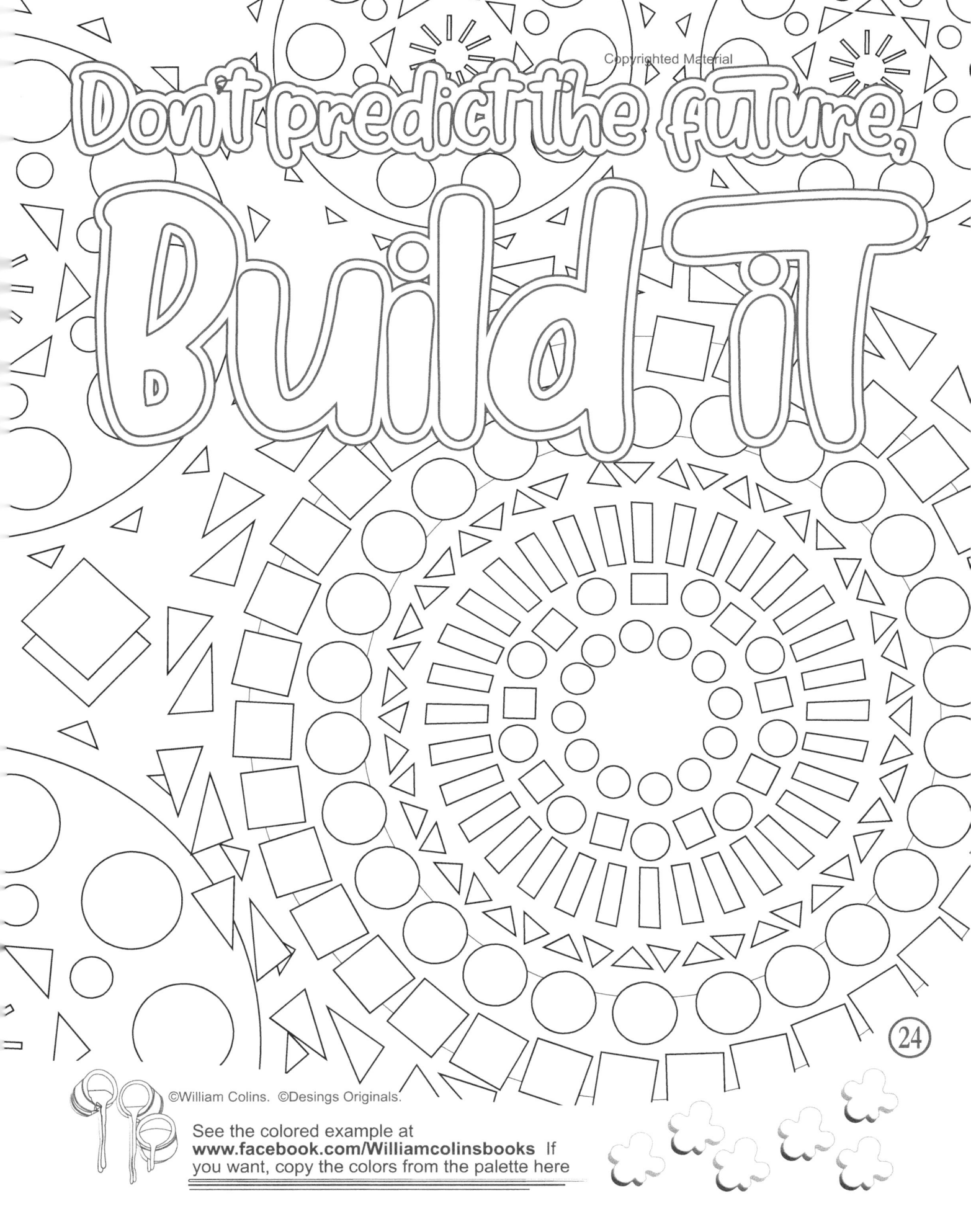

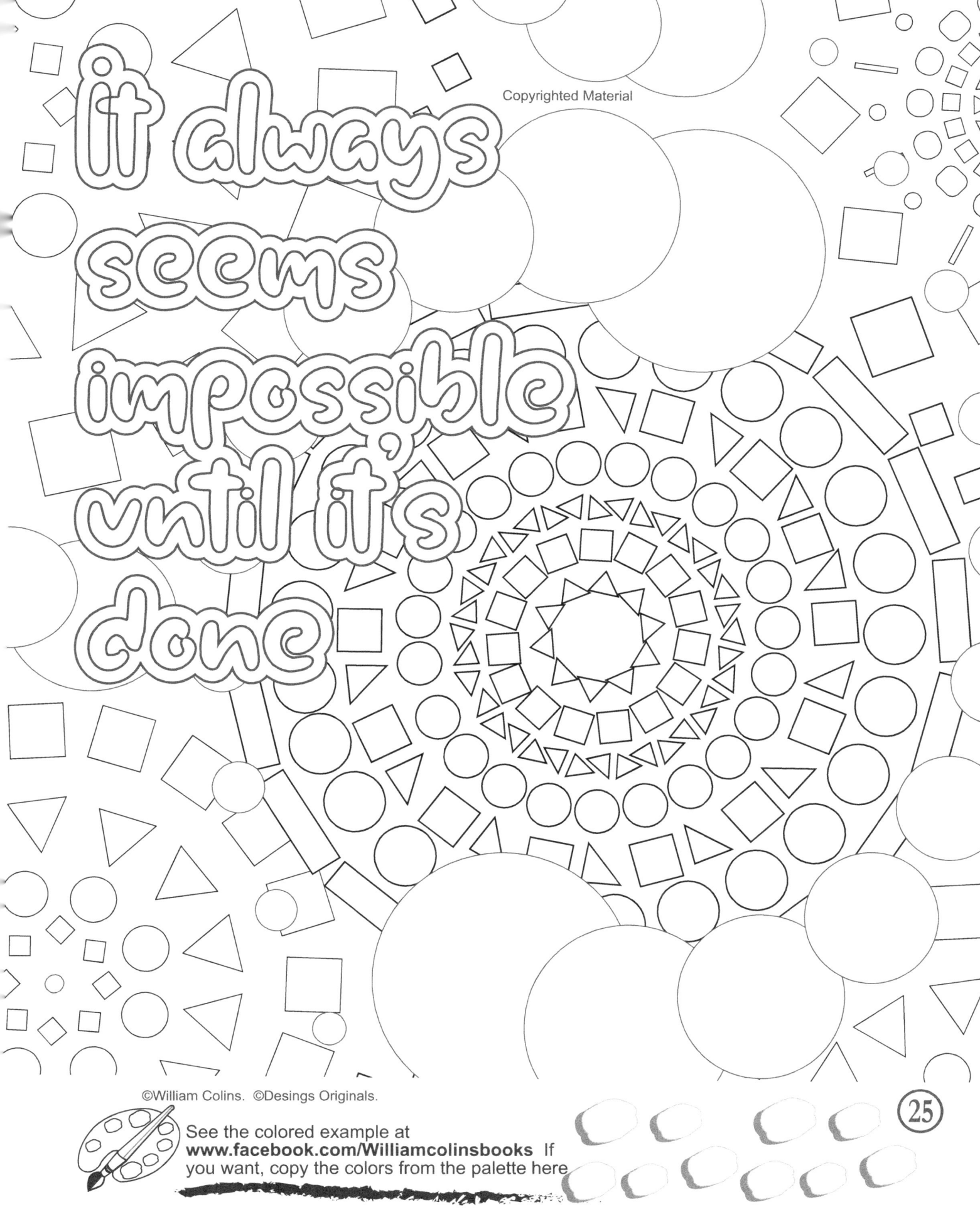

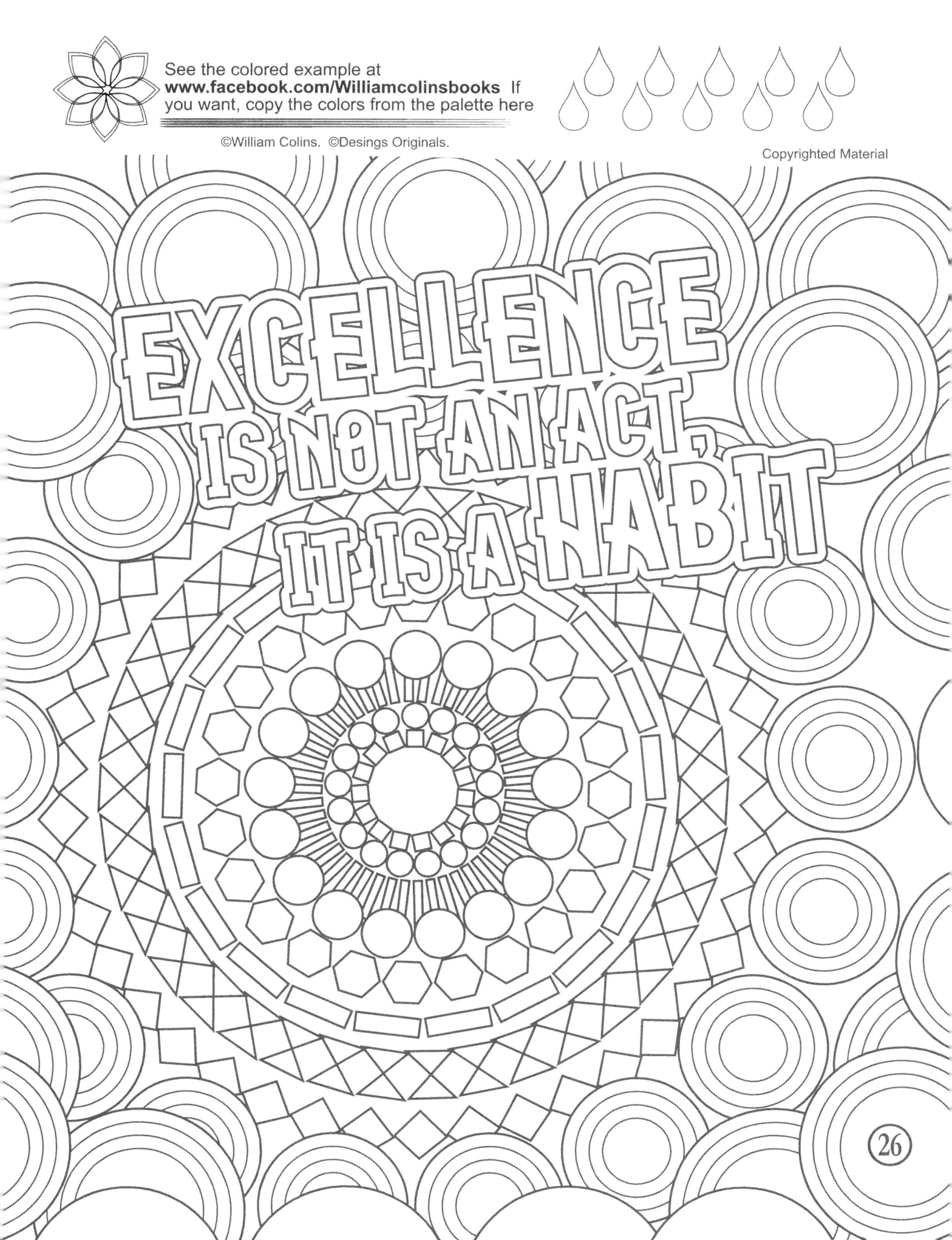

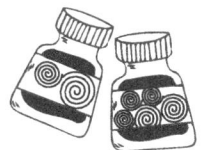 See the colored example at **www.facebook.com/Williamcolinsbooks** If you want, copy the colors from the palette here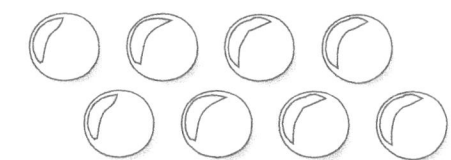

©William Colins. ©Desings Originals. Copyrighted Material

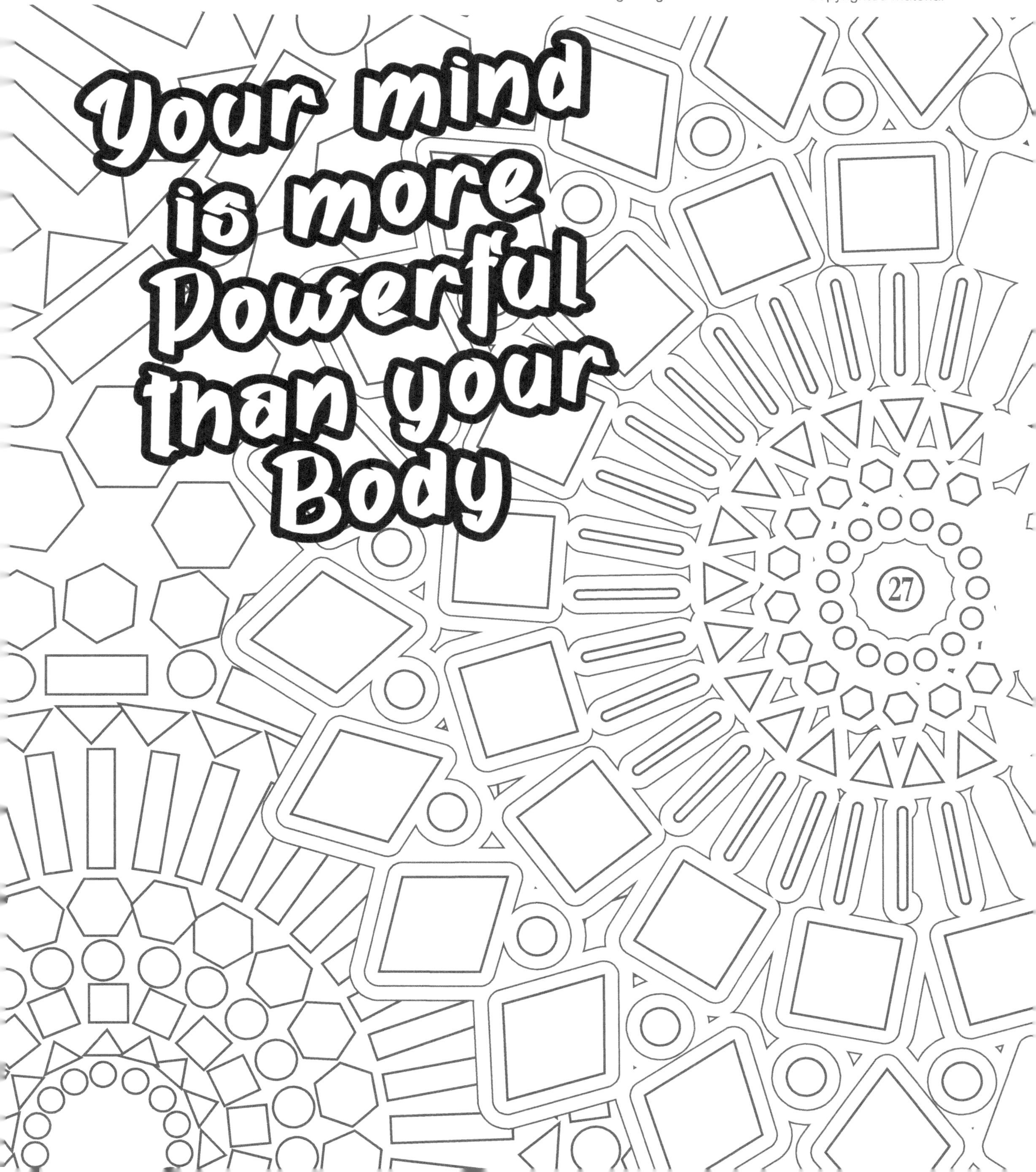

Your mind is more Powerful than your Body

27

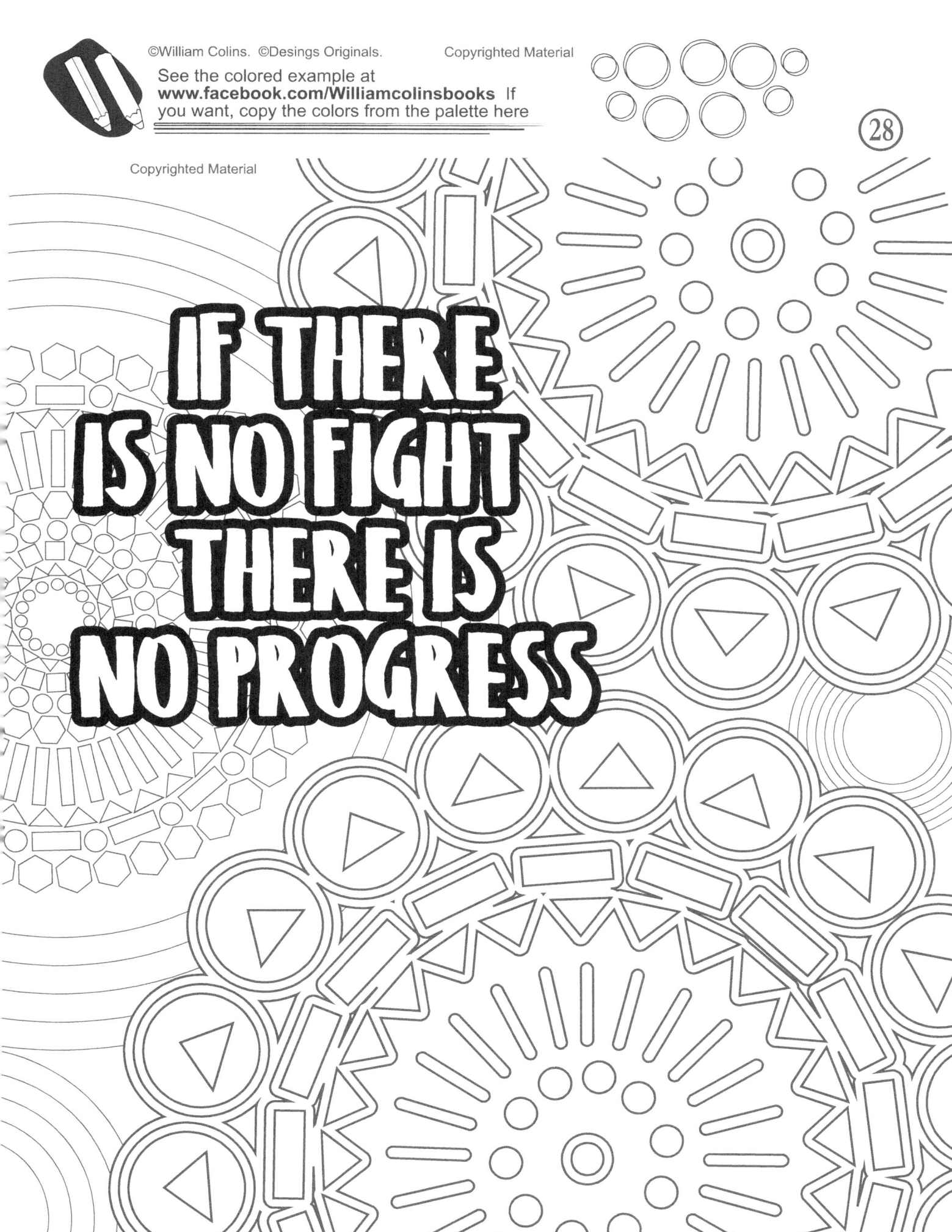

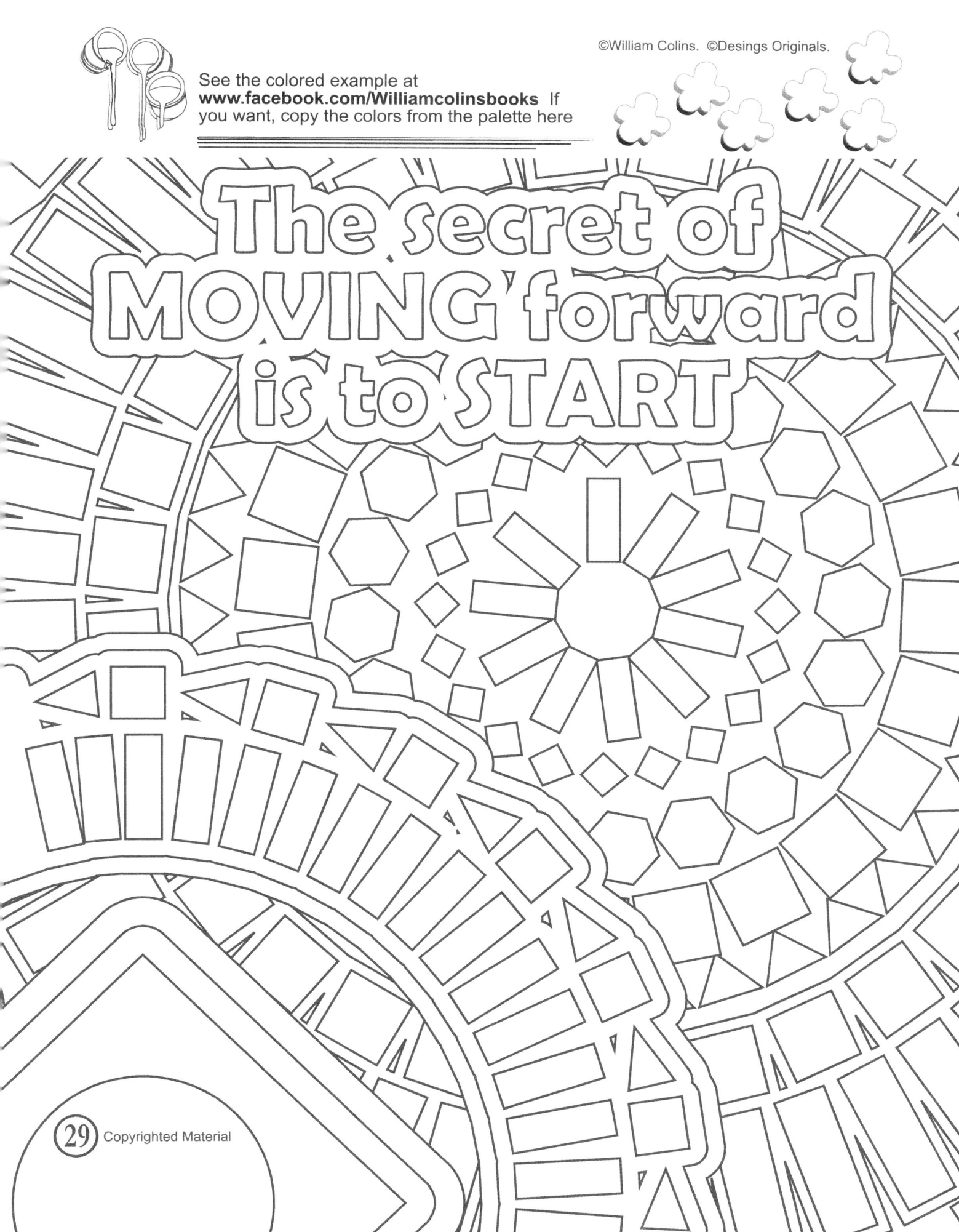

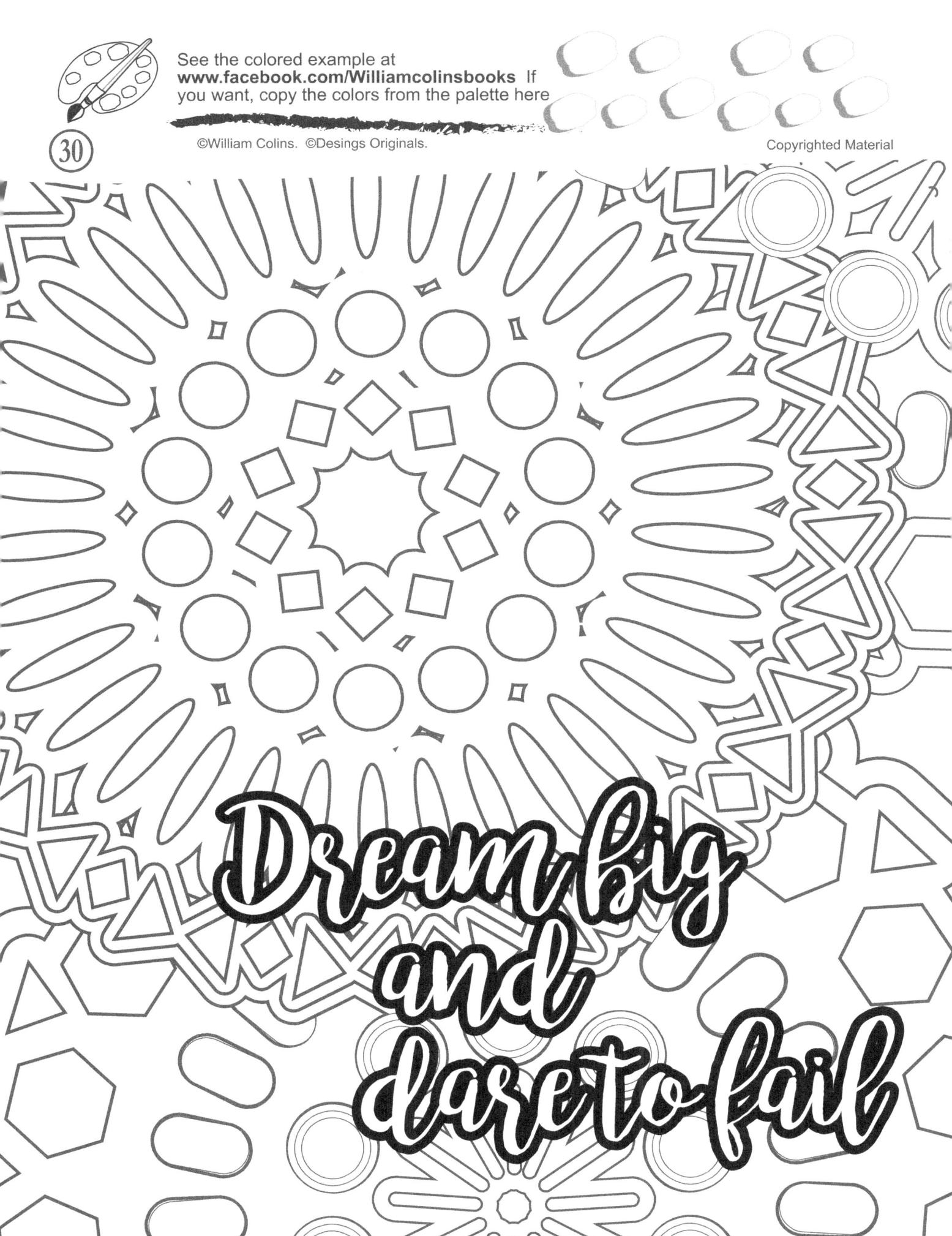

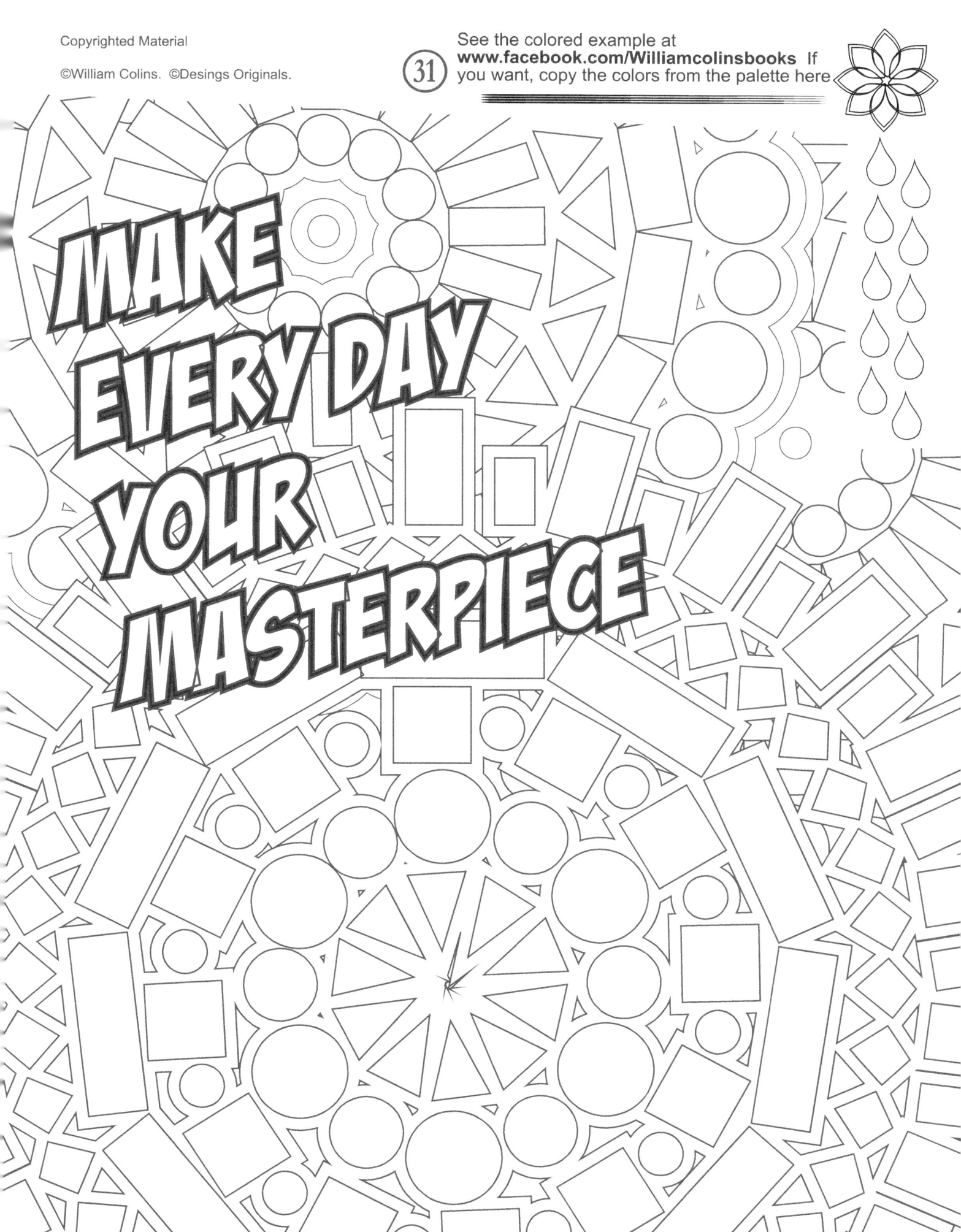

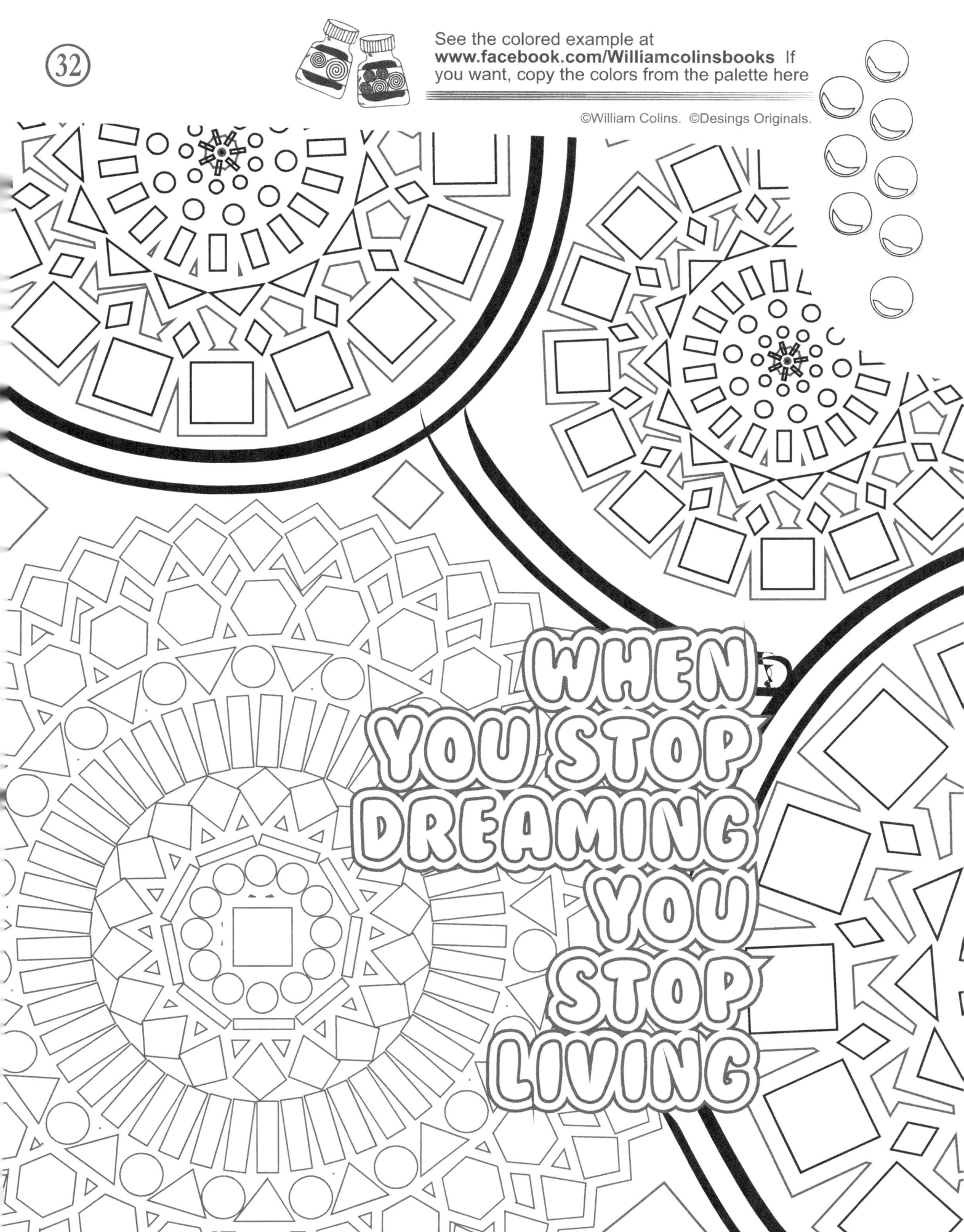

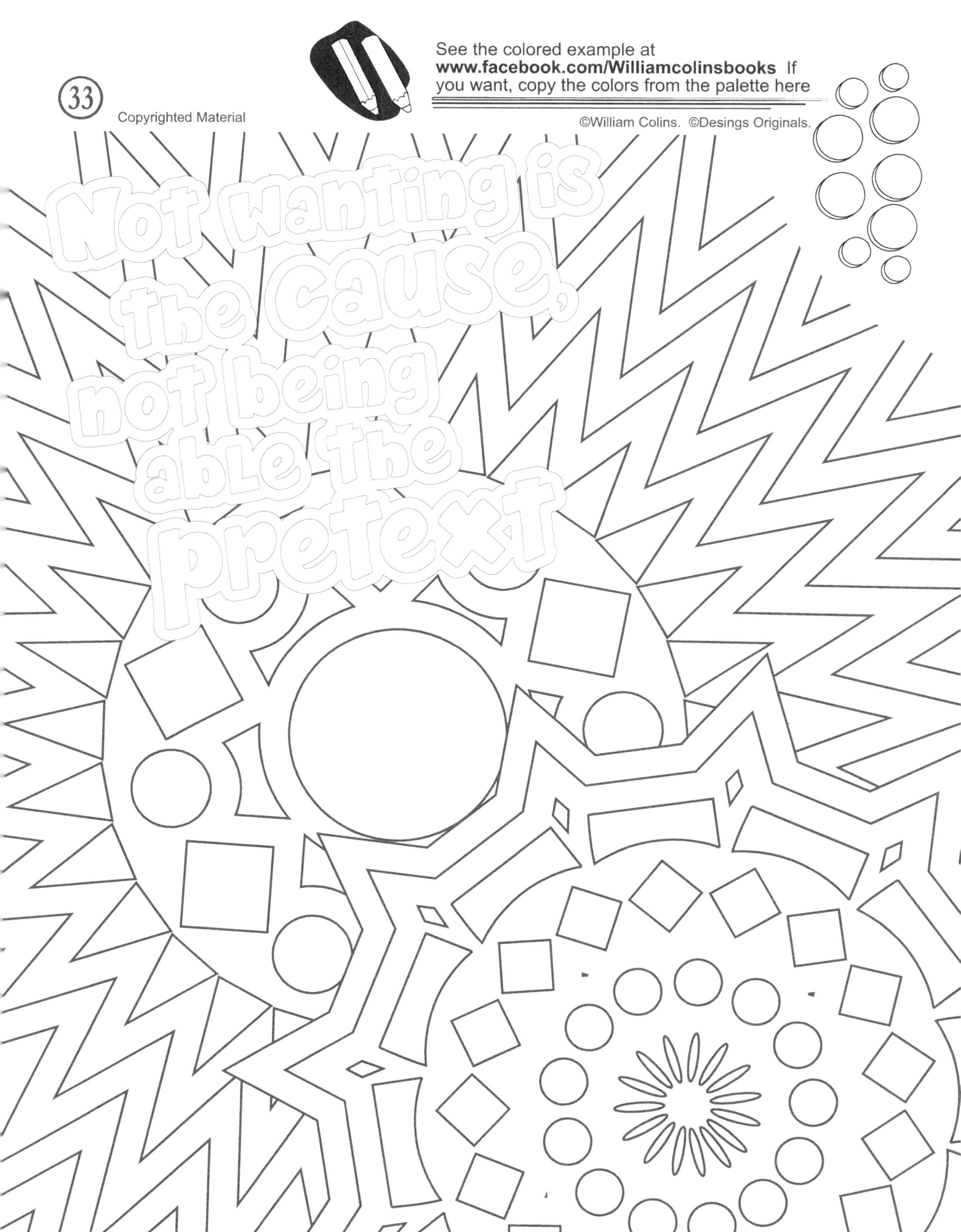

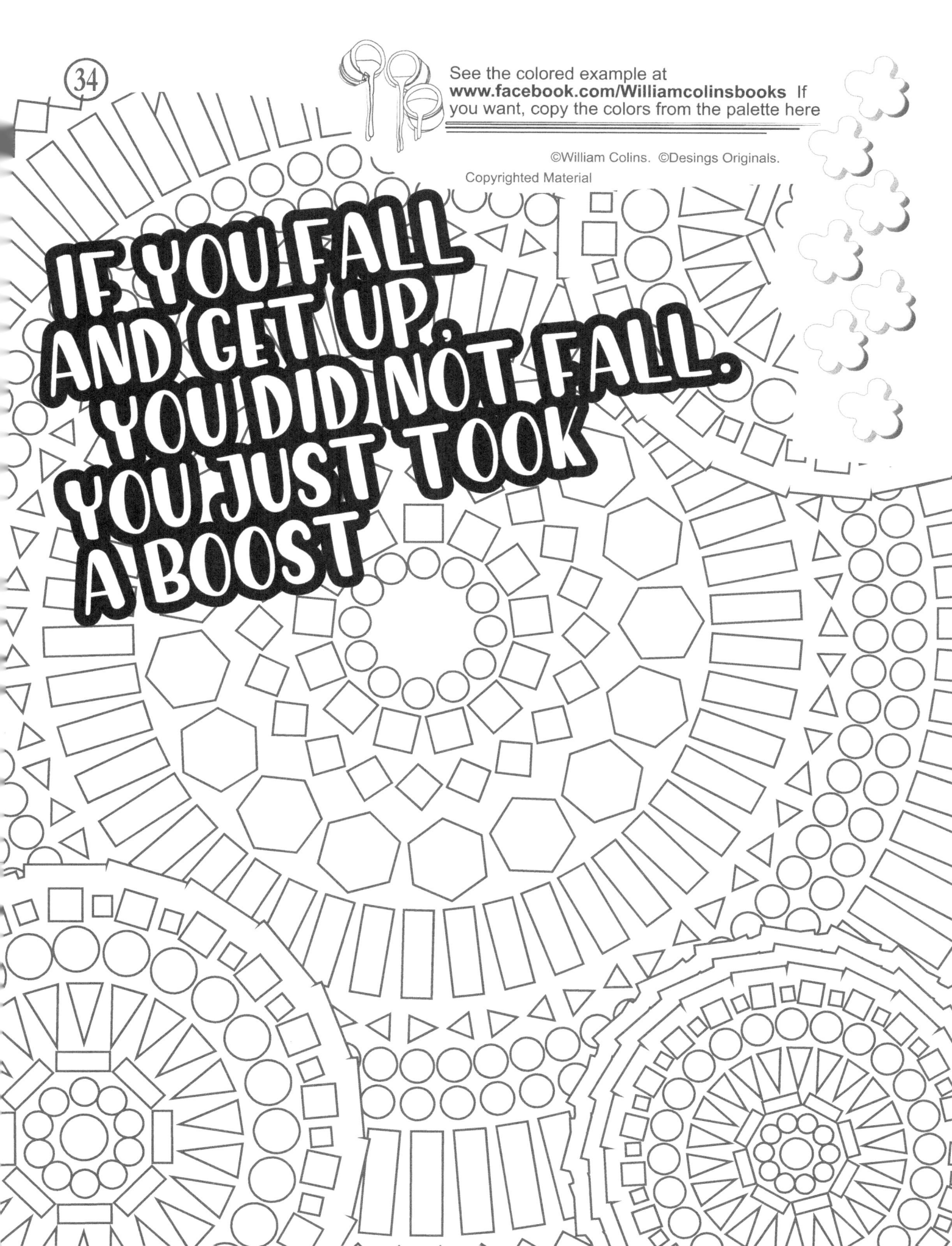

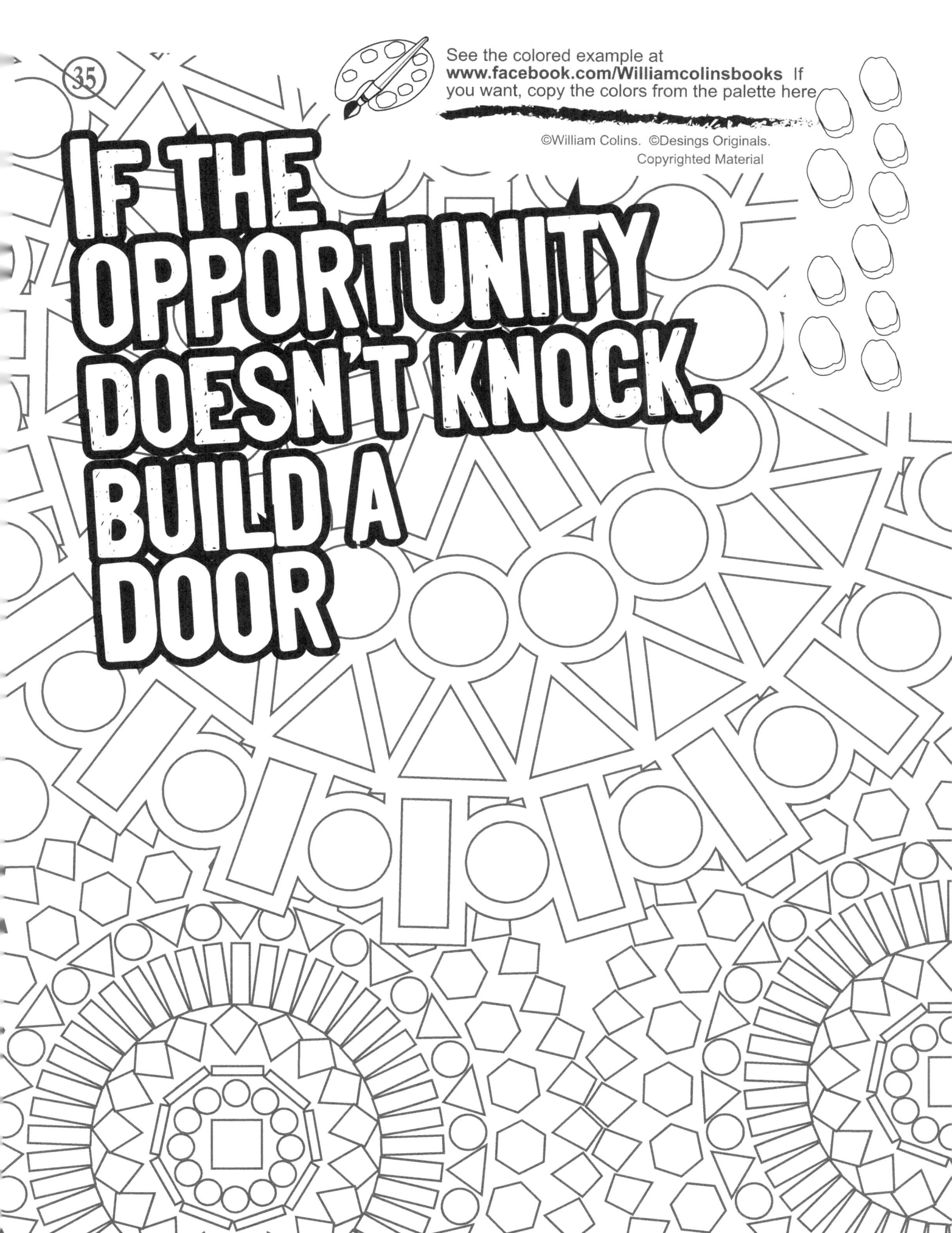

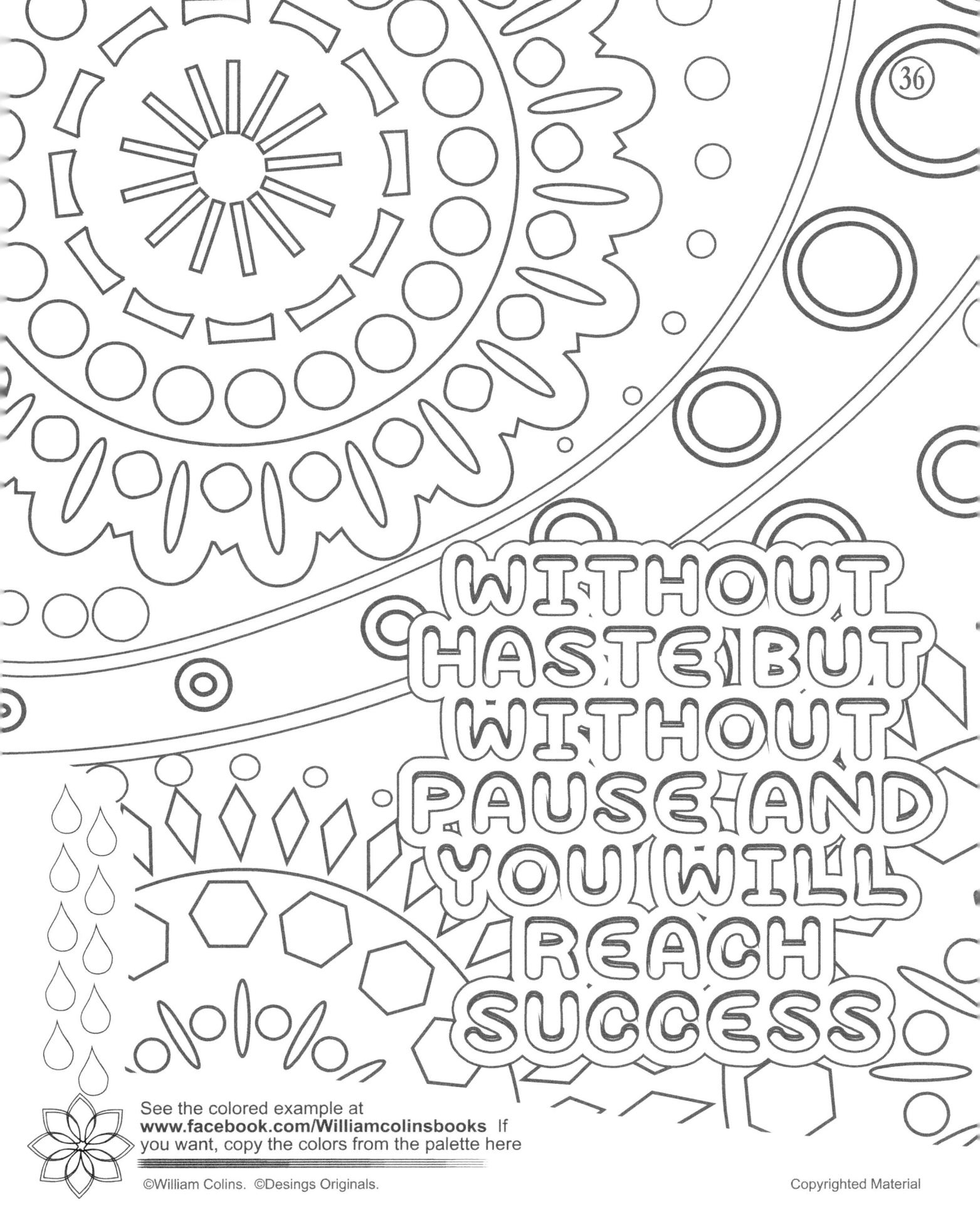

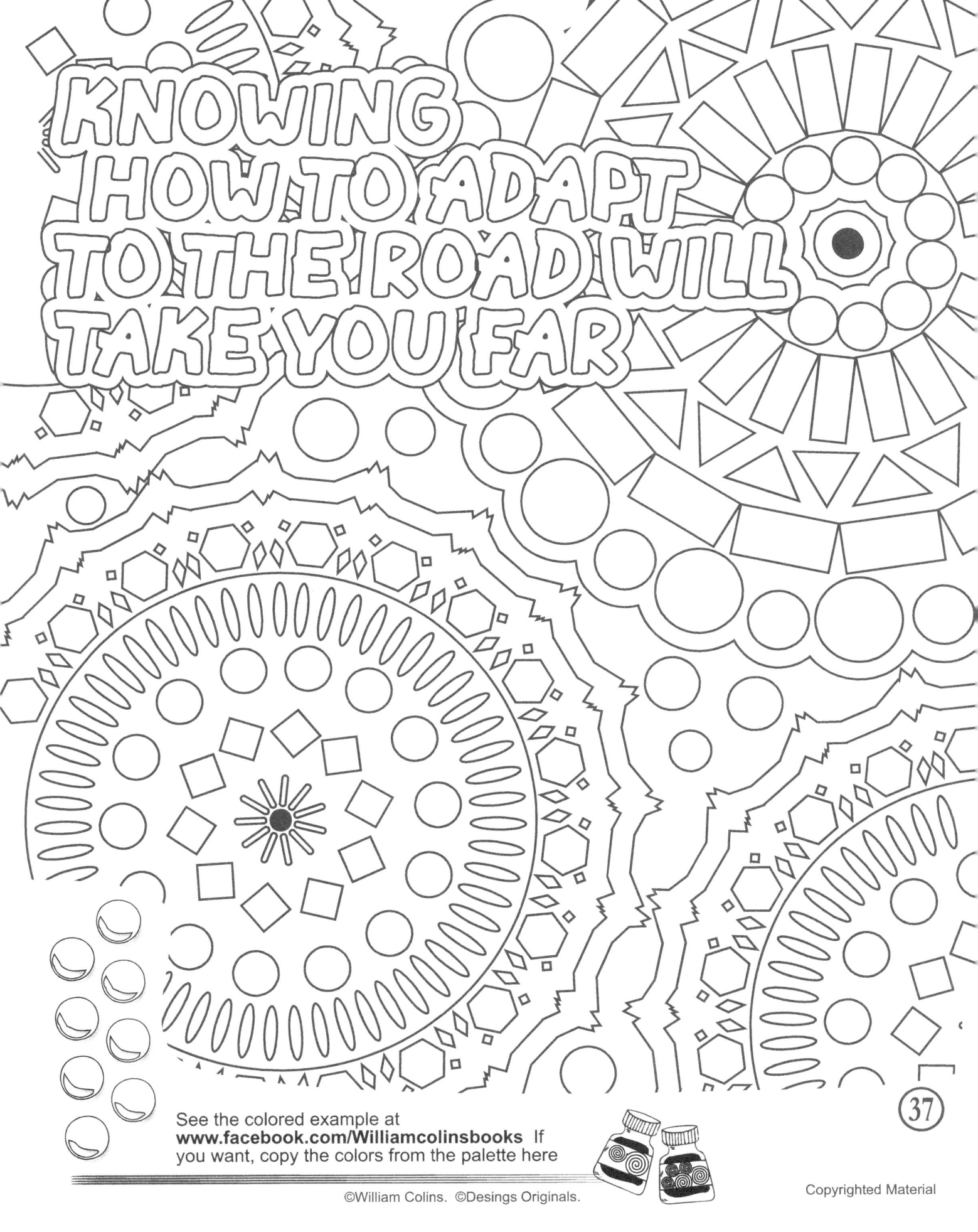

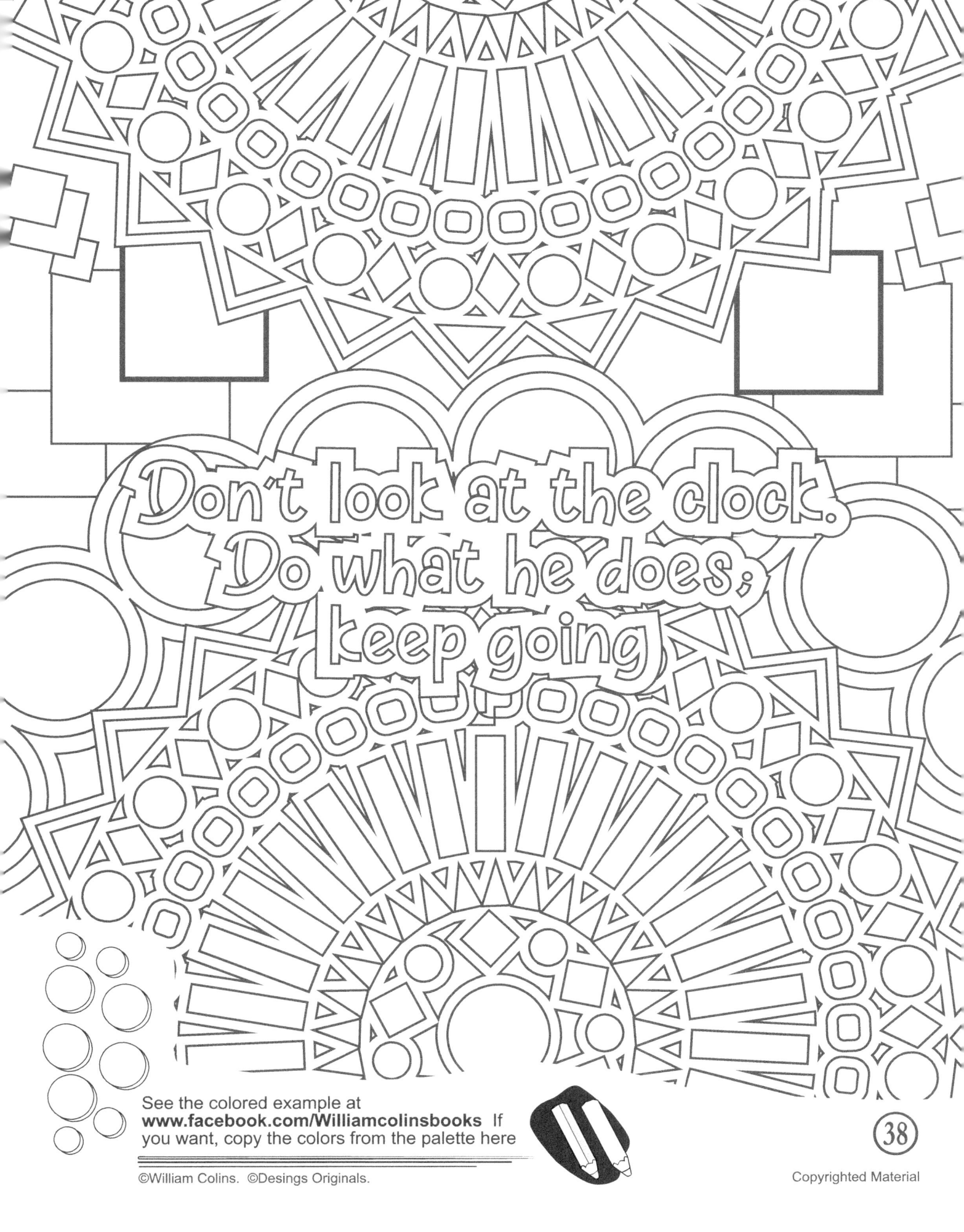

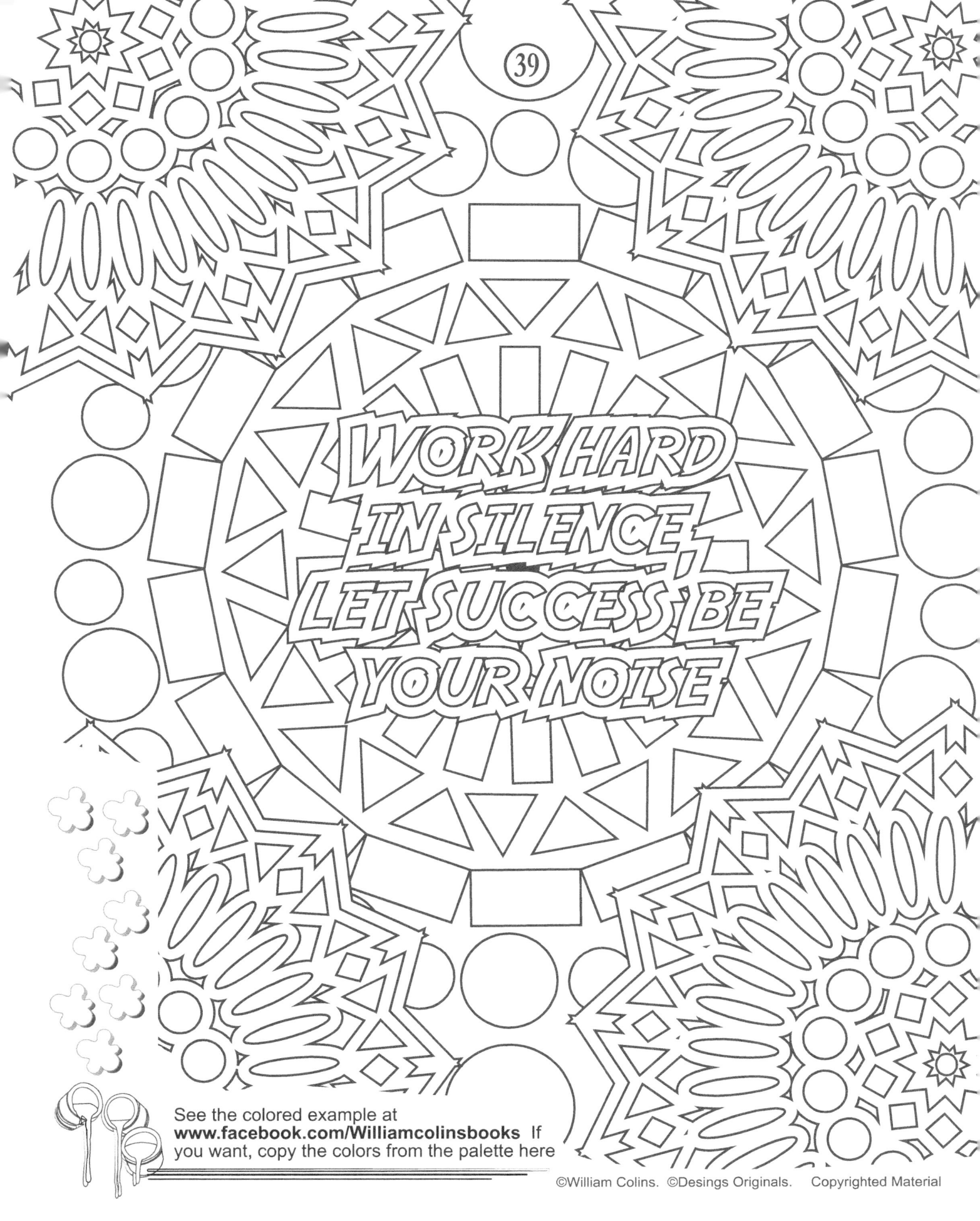

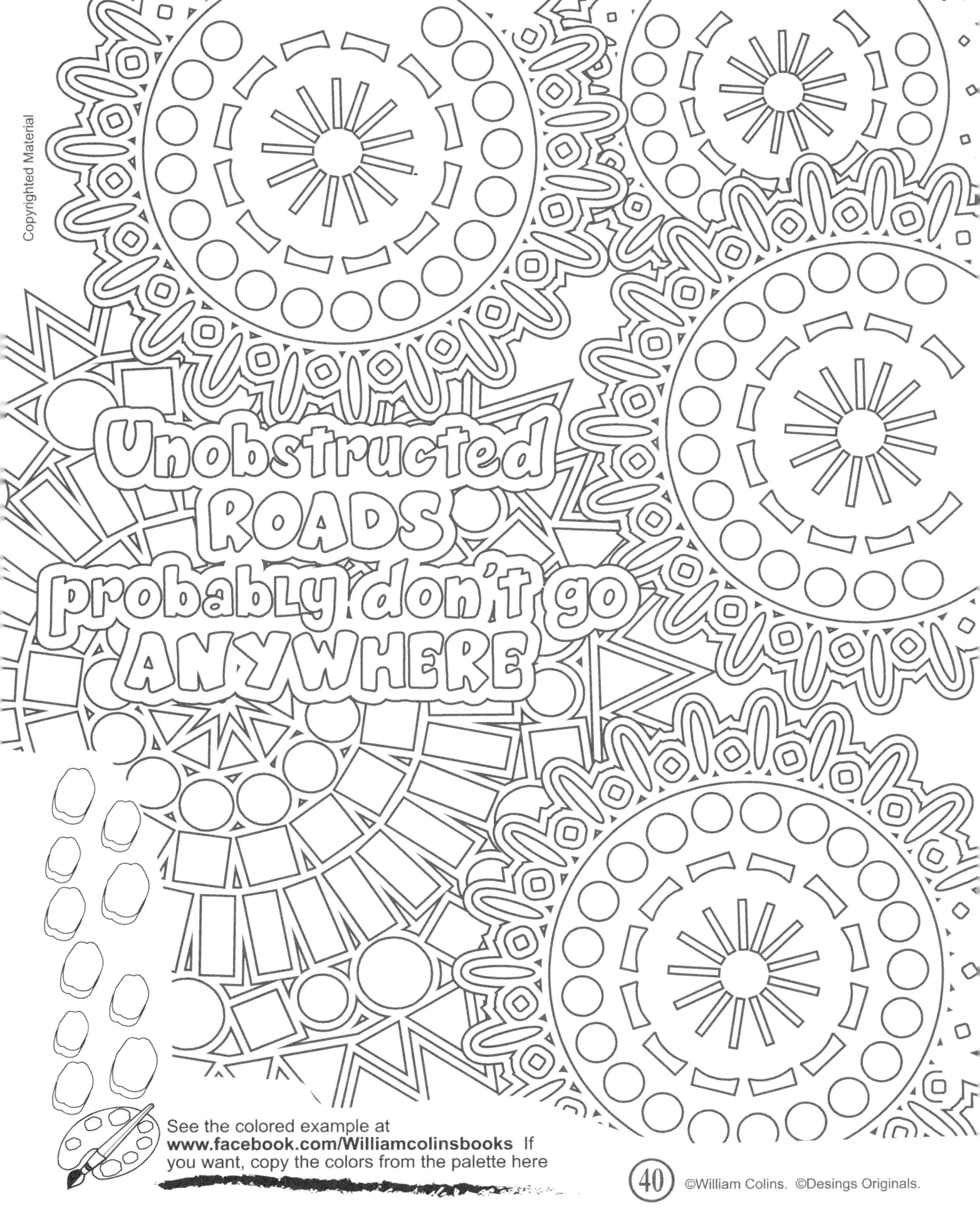

CONCLUSION

In this coloring book for adults with notes, we have managed, in an easy, fun and colorful way, to present forty messages that inspire to lift your spirits and not fall into the difficult difficulties that arise, therefore, look for the positive side.

The magic of colors very well fulfills the character of enjoying time and thus improving the ability to concentrate and have a healthy, calm and very beneficial pastime to release the stress caused by the great complexity of modern life.

We can end by saying that this work was conceived with great analysis to bring tranquility, joy and peace when learning and coloring all its pages and to continue working with the same purpose for future work.

I invite you to look at the colored examples at

www.facebook.com/Williamcolinsbooks

Completely free access to this exclusive content when you buy your book.

Send us or tag us on your painted works.

Thank you.

www.ingramcontent.com/pod-product-compliance
Lightning Source LLC
Chambersburg PA
CBHW060433220526

45465CB00008B/3122